THE
OVERTAXED
INVESTOR

Phil DeMuth

THE
OVERTAXED
INVESTOR

SLASH YOUR
TAX BILL
& BE A TAX
ALPHA DOG

Published by Alpha Dog Press, Los Angeles, California

This publication contains the author's opinions and is intended to provide accurate and authoritative information of a general nature. It is sold with the understanding that the author and publisher are not engaged in rendering specific legal, accounting, investment planning, or other specific professional advice. Any accounting, legal, financial, business, or tax advice construed from its contents is not intended as a thorough, in-depth analysis of specific issues that can substitute for personalized expert opinion. In all cases the reader should seek the services of qualified professionals for this. The author and publisher cannot be held accountable for any loss incurred as a result of specific investment or planning decisions made by the reader.

ISBNs:
Hardcover: 978-0-9970596-2-5
eBook: 978-0-9970596-3-2

First Printing, 2016
Second Edition, 2020

Book Design: 1106 Design
Cover illustration by John Caldwell

Publisher's Cataloging-in-Publication Data
DeMuth, Philip.
The Overtaxed Investor: Slash your tax bill & be a tax-alpha dog / Phil DeMuth. 2nd ed.
p. cm.
ISBN 978-0-9970596-2-5 (hardcover) ISBN 978-0-9970596-3-2 (eBook)
1. Finance, Personal—United States. 2. Taxes—United States I. DeMuth, Phil 1950-. II. Title.

Printed in the United States of America

10 9 8 7 6 5 4 3 2 1

For my clients: God bless them, every one!

Table of
Contents

Chapter One

The Tail of the
Tax Alpha Dog

You want to become a *Tax Alpha Dog.*

Alpha, in investing, means getting excess returns.

Tax Alpha refers to the extra returns you get by not paying more in taxes on your investments than legally required.

The bitter truth is that Certified Public Accountants (CPAs) don't show a lot of love to their tax clients these days. Tax preparation is a small and dwindling part of their business. If you want tax planning advice, you had better be a business client of the tax CPA firm. Otherwise, you are on your own.

This book is about how you can optimize taxes on your investments. Investing is my specialty. If you want to know whether you can deduct your Porsche as a business office, ask somebody else.

This new edition covers the Trump tax cuts, which saved about 2.2% in income taxes overall and simplified estate planning by providing large estate tax exemptions. But if you are a high-income investor, it might have left you worse off. Imagine that you live in an expensive house in a high tax state. You just lost a $100,000 state tax deduction and a $50,000 mortgage tax deduction in exchange for a 2.6% drop in your marginal tax rate. For taxpayers like these, the 2025 expiration of the Trump tax cuts can't come soon enough.

Sometimes a piece of legislation is so terrible that both parties immediately fall in love with it. That was the case with the 2019 Secure Act. As we go to press, it is unclear whether this bill will be enacted into law, so this book will contemplate two alternative future universes: one where the bill passes, and one where it does not.

As written, the Secure Act is an estate planning catastrophe for people with large IRAs. By eliminating the "stretch" IRA, it takes the sensible planning done over the past 20 years and stands it on its head.

The stretch IRA let you leave your IRA to your children or grandchildren, who could then extend the required minimum distributions over their actuarial lifetimes. This payout would be small for a child but would grow over the decades until an inherited IRA would help provide for that child's retirement. A parent would die with the knowledge that whatever vicissitudes their children might experience in life, they would have freedom from want in old age. This is a wonderful legacy, and Congress wants to kill it. In exchange, they let you postpone your first required minimum distribution by either one or two years, depending upon in which month you were born.

The Secure Act is also a catastrophe for middle-class parents sending their kids to college. These temporary jumbo distributions from inherited IRAs will make the families spuriously appear high-income on the Free Application for Federal Student Aid, ruining their chances for need-based financial aid.

The Secure Act lowers the value of all types of retirement plans—perhaps not for the 44% of the population who pay no Federal income taxes, but probably for you. The fact that it was slated to pass both houses of Congress with near-unanimous votes, with no debate, and included a stealth tax of about 30% on inherited IRAs, proves that the government cannot be trusted to keep its word and respect private ownership of our retirement plans. These plans need to be approached warily going forward.

The Tail and the Dog

When it comes to investing, people focus on the wrong thing: chasing returns. People search for the mysterious and elusive alpha from investment performance, the latest hot stock, the manager with the hot hand, but this is counter-productive and usually amounts to an exercise in frustration. Meanwhile, taxes are certain, as real as the concrete pavement under our feet. Tax strategy is entirely within our power. We can put our hands on the controls and determine the outcome. Taxes beat alpha. People would be wealthier if they indexed their investments and got their alpha from tax management instead.

As Cambria's Meb Faber says, "while most people spend 90% of the time thinking about allocation, what they should be spending 90% of the time on—if they're doing buy-and-hold—is minimizing fees and minimizing taxes." Or take this tip from the Capital Spectator's Jim Picerno: "Everyone wants to earn higher returns and excel in all things financial. But for most folks, there's more opportunity on the negative side of money management: reducing if not eliminating the mistakes."

A review of the field finds that "the typical approach for managing taxable portfolios, acting as if the taxes cannot be reduced or deferred, remains the industry standard." The report concludes, "most managers' alpha [excess return over the benchmark] does not cover their clients' tax bill."

Under President Trump's Tax Cut and Jobs Act (hereafter, TCJA), high-income investors pay 23.8% tax on their dividends and long-term capital gains. This includes the 20% Federal tax plus the 3.8% Affordable Care Act "Obamacare" Net Investment Income Tax. State taxes are on top of this. In California, state taxes top out at 13.3%, for a total of 36.8%. Other high-taxing states include Hawaii (11%), Oregon (9.9%) Minnesota (9.85%), Iowa (8.98%), and New York (8.82%).

You may have heard the platitude, "don't let the tax tail wag the investment dog." Investment advisors trot this out when confronted with some tax-saving suggestion that would cramp their style. Translation: "Our investment philosophy is so fabulous that it will swamp these few pennies you are concerned about." Or, more briefly, "Don't bother us."

When advisors say, "Our approach is inherently tax-efficient," this usually translates, "Um, tax strategy—what, me worry?" Taxes always seem to be the other guy's problem. But who pays them? You do, dear reader. You are that other guy.

It used to be that you could start with a diversified portfolio and then put on a tax overlay. Not anymore. Today you start with taxes, and only after your investments have made it through the tax screen do you put them in a diversified portfolio. If you are in a high bracket and have no way to defuse some tax-inefficient investment, your best course is usually to avoid it altogether. Otherwise, to make it work, you need to assume it will have a super high level of future returns. Is this realistic?

It used to be that you could wing it year-by-year, doing whatever lowered your taxes the most right now. This is sub-optimal. There are times when you are better off paying more taxes (at lower rates) today.

Sadly, people shovel far more money into the open maw of the Internal Revenue Service than they need to because they don't know how to do a few things correctly with their investments.

Caveat Emptor

You need to run the ideas in this book by your own tax and investment advisors before acting. Taxes are about following rules, which can be ever-shifting and open to new interpretations. I will post the inevitable mistakes on my web page (www.phildemuth.com).

Coming Attractions

To start, we need to understand the three types of investment accounts and which assets to park in each one.

Then we visit the ammunition depot to survey the various legal methods that investors use to lower their tax bills, especially high-net-worth investors.

Armed with this information, we walk through your life by stages, to see how investment taxes apply over the life cycle—while you are working, when you are retired, and during that intriguing but little-appreciated period between retirement and the time when Social Security and the Required Minimum Distributions from your tax-deferred accounts begin. The goal is to ride the brackets over your lifetime like a buckaroo.

After that, we're going to spend some time talking about zero-dividend stock investing, a special interest of mine. If you are a high-bracket taxpayer with money in a taxable account, this can be life-changing.

Finally, for the sake of completeness, we will sign off with a few deathless remarks about estate planning.

The Boneyard

- We pay a small fortune in taxes, and yet we are not getting much help. We are all in this alone.

- As investors, we are far better off focusing on things we can control, such as taxes, instead of on things we cannot control, like our future returns, whatever they will be.

- The tax alpha dog focuses on reducing his tax bill over his lifetime, not just this year.

- Tax management is too important to be a mere after-thought after all other investment decisions have been made. By then, it's too late. The new rule is: start with taxes.

- Check http://phildemuth.com/ for any horrific mistakes.

Chapter Two

The Three Bowls of Investment Accounts
and What to Put in Each

The simplest way to become a tax alpha dog is to set up and fund the right accounts with the right assets. You only need to do it once. The higher your taxes, and the longer your investment horizon, the more you will benefit.

Here are three bowls of investment accounts, classified according to their unique tax status.

Taxable Accounts: Tax Me Now!

Taxable accounts contain income that will be taxed in the current year. This income might include interest, dividends, and capital gains, each taxed at its own rate. The principal itself always remains untaxed.

When you walk in the door to set up an investment account, you are presented with twenty pages of paperwork with boxes to check and blanks to fill in. Because the earnest young man in the ill-fitting suit is waiting across the desk, you answer his questions as best you can off the top of your head and sign on the last page, never to read the fine print or think about these choices again. The earnest young man wants to collect your check and sees no need to dwell on the details, which he does not particularly understand anyway.

Unfortunately, these details are nontrivial.

At the most basic level, how is your account registered? Bang, we are off and running with an item with far-reaching consequences. It determines who owns and controls the assets, who can sell them, whom creditors can go after, and what happens to the assets after you have entered the great beyond.

Is the account registered to you as an individual? Hmm.

Right away, I see that you don't have a revocable trust. Which means that if you die, the money in this account will go through probate, a needlessly prolonged and costly legal process that is also public. When J.P. Morgan died in 1913 with an estate worth $1.2 billion in today's dollars, J.D. Rockefeller remarked, "And to think—he wasn't even a wealthy man." Don't let people gossip like this about your estate.

It would be better to plate your account in the name of your revocable trust. Of course, this means you need to set up the trust in the first place.

Possibly you are married, and the account contains joint assets? Fine, but then there are even more choices to weigh. If it is registered to both of you, shouldn't it be registered to your revocable trust or trusts? If the account is in both your names, often one person is legally responsible (his or her Social Security number is on the account), while the other party can sign on the account but is not a legal owner. Is that what you intend?

Another arrangement could be *joint tenants with right of survivorship* (JTWROS) or a *transfer on death* (TOD) account. If one owner dies, the other owner gets the proceeds outside of probate, bypassing your will entirely.

Some states also offer the option of owning by *Tenancy in the Entirety,* which gives better asset protection if one owner is sued. The death of one party does not mean the other party inherits the property: it goes into the estate of the deceased and is disposed of according to his or her will. The same is true of the *Tenants in Common* registration: the proceeds do not go to the other person unless the will of the deceased says so. There are pros and cons to each registration.

In other words, you need to investigate the best way to title your assets. If you are twenty-five and single with $4,000 in the bank, it doesn't matter, but if you are forty-five and married with children, this discussion is overdue. You can't know the correct way to title your assets until you have consulted an attorney about your estate.

Here we are just out of the gate, and I'm saying to get lawyered up. But you're not dying. For now, recognize that these details have far-flung implications, put this on your "to-do" list, and let's get back to taxes.

Cost Basis Reporting

Your *cost basis* is the price you originally paid for the assets you hold. While this might seem straightforward, there's more to it than meets the eye. When you are buying and selling securities in a brokerage account, you need to tell your custodian which method to use to report your cost basis to the IRS, because you will owe capital gains taxes on any profits.

Imagine that over the years, you accumulated one thousand shares of Apple Computer, and this year you sell two hundred of them. Which two hundred shares did you sell?

Here are your choices. Hint: you probably have the first one.

☐ *First In, First Out (FIFO)*. They will assume you sold the first shares you bought and use their price as your cost basis. This is the default method used by the IRS for stocks. Don't use it.

☐ *Average Cost Basis*. They will take the average price of all the shares you purchased and apply that average price to each share you sell. This is the default method used by mutual fund companies. Don't use it. Once you do, you are stuck with it forever.

☐ *Specific Share Identification*. You tell them which shares you are selling and specify them by the trade's settlement date. It is a pain to do this manually every time you make a sale, so eventually, you will forget. Move your account to a custodian that gives you better choices.

For example, Fidelity and Schwab add choices like these:

☐ *Last In, First Out (LIFO)*. They will assume that you sold the shares you most recently purchased and use that price as your cost basis. It is used by law when you take a distribution from some annuities. Otherwise, don't use it.

☐ *Low Cost.* They will sell your least expensive shares first, which should give you the highest possible higher tax bill. Believe it or not, there can be reasons to do this, as we will see later. But ordinarily, run from this.

☐ *High Cost.* They will sell your most expensive shares first, which should give you a lower tax bill. This is the choice you want unless they offer:

☐ *Tax Sensitive,* or

☐ *Tax Lot Optimizer,* or

☐ *Best Tax*

The last three choices are different names for the same accounting method, the one invariably preferred by the sophisticated tax alpha dog. They sell your short-term losses first, then your long-term losses, then your long-term gains, and finally your short-term gains, in that order. It should result in your paying the lowest taxes on your trades, always deferring the bigger taxes to some tax Tomorrowland.

Dividend and Capital Gain Reinvestment

There is one more account-opening question that applies to all types of investment accounts. Do you want your dividend and capital gain distributions paid out in cash to your account, or do you want them reinvested in the securities that issued them? By default, everything will be reinvested. Is that smart?

If you are retired and spending the money, you want them paid out in cash. If you are young and have the money in a few molar index funds or a target-date fund, you want them reinvested (to put your money to work immediately and save on commissions). If your investments are diversified among various asset classes and sub-asset classes, then you will prefer to have the distributions paid in cash so you can periodically rebalance among them. It makes no difference, tax-wise—you will pay taxes on the distributions no matter which choice you make.

That's it for setting up your taxable accounts: register them appropriately, choose the best capital gains setting, and select your preferred reinvestment options. But before putting so much as a dollar in a taxable account, ask yourself whether you should put that same dollar in a tax-deferred account instead.

Tax-Deferred Accounts: Tax Me Later!

These are retirement savings accounts available to anyone with earned income. They include your 401(k) plan at work (or a 403(b) plan for a teacher or a 457 plan for a government employee) or your traditional or SEP or rollover Individual Retirement Account (IRA). These contain money that has not been taxed yet, but that will be taxed as ordinary income when you withdraw it from the account in the future.

You own these accounts in partnership with Uncle Sam, who is letting grow value untaxed while you are working but who will take his cut once you retire. You can take withdrawals penalty-free at age 59½, and if the Secure Act passes, you may postpone taking mandatory distributions until age 72—otherwise, per current law, they have to start at age 70½.

Retirement accounts are registered to you as an individual. Unlike with taxable accounts, though, you are asked to name *beneficiaries* for these accounts in the event of your demise. You will want to designate a person as a beneficiary, not your estate or your trust unless your attorney has drafted a special trust with stretch provisions for the express purpose of receiving these assets. If the Secure Act has passed, even that may be a bad idea. See the last chapter on estate taxes for more on this contingency.

You also want to name *secondary beneficiaries*. They will inherit the account in the event your primary beneficiary no longer wants it or is not alive. Here's an idea that covers a lot of cases: make the primary beneficiary your spouse and the secondary beneficiaries your children.

CPA Ed Slott reports the biggest issue with retirement plans is that people don't have the beneficiary paperwork filed correctly. Retirement plans do not pass through your estate; they go where the plan paperwork says. Do your plans reflect your current intentions—with both primary and secondary beneficiaries listed? You won't know for sure unless you check. Here's the best advice you will read in this chapter: put the book down and log into your retirement accounts right now to make sure the beneficiaries are set correctly.

If the Secure Act has passed, it will force nearly all non-spouse beneficiaries to pull out the money from your inherited IRA over ten years. This change has made employee plans and Traditional IRAs a less desirable bequest. A surviving spouse can pull out the money over his or her actuarial lifetime (or yours, if that is preferable). Your child (but not your grandchild) under age 21 can pull it out over his or her actuarial lifetime until age 21, and then the 10-year clock starts for them as well. Beneficiaries who are disabled, chronically ill, or fewer than ten years younger than the original account owner are exempt from this provision.

Sooner or later, your IRA will likely pass to your adult children. If a million-dollar IRA ends up in the hands of an attorney/daughter, she will have to add $100,000 of annual income on top of her six-figure salary for a decade under the Secure Act. Perhaps half of it will be swallowed by taxes.

Imagine you remarry. You think you have protected your kids' inheritance by making them the primary beneficiaries of your million-dollar 401(k). But when you die a few weeks later, your new wife's attorney informs her that she has first claim on these assets. Because you failed to get her to sign a waiver, the 401(k) goes to your new bride, leaving your children like baby robins without a worm. As estate attorney Jonathan Blattmachr has observed, "Everybody hates a surviving spouse younger than the kids, especially one named after a woodland creature."

Tax-Free Accounts: Tax Me Never Again!

Finally, there are post-tax Roth accounts. These assets will never be taxed again. The Roth force field deflects all taxes.

In 2020, you can only make Roth IRA contributions if your income is under $139,000 single/$206,000 married (here and forever after, when I say "married," I mean "married filing jointly"). You pay taxes on the money before it goes into the account, but after that the money compounds tax-free. After the dollars marinate in the account for at least five years and you are over 59½, you can pull out the interest and earnings tax- and penalty-free. These five years began January 1 of the year you make your first contribution. You are free to pull the original contributions out tax-free whenever you want.

In 2006, the Roth 401(k) came into existence, allowing workers to put up to $19,500 a year inside a Roth wrapper. Workers over age 50 can contribute $26,000.

Historically, the people who qualified for Roth IRAs didn't need them, while the people who needed them couldn't get them. Then in 2010, Congress—strapped for wampum—opened Roth IRAs to anyone willing to pay taxes today to convert their traditional IRAs into Roths, including people whose high earnings disqualified them from opening a Roth in the first place. High earners could not invest in a Roth, but they could invest in a Traditional IRA and then convert it.

The ability to withdraw Roth money tax-free lets people fine-tune their income in retirement by dipping into the Roth as needed when they want to stay in a low tax tier. Roth withdrawals do not increase the taxability of your Social

Security distributions or Medicare premiums and may help you avoid recognizing capital gains in your taxable account to generate income.

Despite this, few people are willing to write an enormous up-front check to the U.S. Treasury for the privilege of converting a traditional IRA to a Roth. Some think Congress will renege on its promise and tax these accounts, directly or indirectly, with the threatened Secure Act representing a major step in this direction. Under its dictates, the person inheriting the Roth must pull all the money out in ten years, instead of being allowed to spread the distributions over their lifetime.

If you will become a high earner someday, your last best chance to establish a Roth on the cheap will be when you are starting your career and still in a low bracket. Your spouse is the ideal primary beneficiary for a Roth because she can inherit it without any obligation to take distributions.

Which Type of Retirement Account Should You Prefer?

It is always advantageous to fund your 401(k) at least up to the level of the employer match. This is free money.

If your tax rate this year looks like it will be higher than the tax rate will be during the years when the money is pulled out, a Traditional IRA or 401(k) or 403(b) or 457 Plan will be the most economically advantageous choice. Most of us expect to pay taxes at higher rates while we are working than after we retire, so this is the most likely choice.

Nonetheless, many people change brackets during retirement. A surviving spouse who inherits your IRA probably will be filing single in a higher tax bracket. If the IRA eventually goes to the kids, consider how much they might be withdrawing every year and what their tax brackets might be then. State taxes count, too. If you live in a high-income tax state today but retire to a low-tax state (say, moving from New York to Florida), your taxes in retirement might be considerably lower.

If your tax rates when you pull the money out are the same as when you put the money in, there is no inherent advantage to a Traditional vs. a Roth IRA. This is the exciting Commutative Law of Multiplication in action. If your tax rate today is the same or lower than the tax rate tomorrow, either the Roth or the taxable account is preferable to the Traditional IRA. See the pros and cons in Table 2.1.

The conventional wisdom would be to put the money in a Roth. Nevertheless, it is not a tragedy if you put the money in your pocket instead, perhaps using it to buy a zero-dividend stock like Berkshire Hathaway. I will have more to say about zero-dividend investing later. There are scenarios where either choice might prove more advantageous.

TABLE 2.1: ROTH VS. TAXABLE		
	Roth IRA	Taxable Zero-Dividend
Pros	No taxes Better asset protection Does not affect SS taxes Does not affect Medicare Surtax	No taxes IF zero-dividend investing No special IRS rules to follow Capital loss harvesting allowed Transfers through estate with step-up in basis
Cons	Follow IRS rules Special estate planning Might be taxed in future	More limited investment choices for zero tax Probable cap gains taxes if entire account is consumed Congress could eliminate capital gains step up

No one knows the optimal balance to hold among tax-deferred, Roth, and taxable accounts. In practice, the more money you make, the more money will overflow the contribution limits of your retirement accounts and spill into your taxable accounts. If your taxable accounts are going to be invested conventionally and not with scrupulous tax efficiency, they should be funded after Roth accounts because they will get a tax trim every year on interest, dividends, and capital gains.

The Insecure Future

All these ideas are based on predictions about future tax rates. No one knows what these will be. Congress giveth and Congress taketh away. People didn't think Social Security benefits would be taxed, but then one day in 1983, they were. While most people foresee higher taxes (even beyond those already on the books for 2026) as our country needs to pay for its ever-expanding and underfunded entitlement programs, it is hard to predict what form these tax increases might take.

Ed Slott does not think Congress will tax Roth accounts (effectively killing them) because doing so would stop the tax revenues that come from people paying to convert their Traditional IRAs to Roths every year. Politicians are unlikely to forego the income today from all these IRA conversions to solve a problem for their successors down the road.

There are half-way measures, though. Congress could add Roth distributions to adjusted gross income (as they did with municipal bond income). This could trigger higher taxes on Social Security payments and raise Medicare premiums and the threshold for the 3.8% Obamacare surtax, all making Roth IRAs less valuable. Roth assets could be subject to confiscation with a general "wealth" tax. Congress could require them to be annuitized, so the Roth benefits disappear sooner.

For taxable accounts, Congress could repeal the capital gains reset to fair market value at death. Some politicians have even suggested that unrealized capital gains be taxed annually. This is not easy to do, but if the government runs out of money and foreign investors are no longer willing to prop up the national debt, anything is possible. The Secure Act illustrates how the government regards our retirement savings accounts as a giant piggy bank, but taxing unrealized capital gains is far more problematic and probably unconstitutional.

More drastically, if we scrapped the income tax for a consumption tax or a value-added tax (VAT), it means Roth investors missed the tax deductions they could have taken had they funded traditional IRAs and 401(k)s instead. Roth holders would be taxed on their income a second time as they spend it.

Federal programs tend to be additive. It is likely that we would not replace our current progressive income tax, but rather pile a Euro-style VAT or a national sales tax on top. The addition of a VAT would mean that the rising income tax rates that motivated Roth investors to pay their taxes today instead of tomorrow would never materialize.

Politicians will do whatever is expedient. If these changes come in response to a crisis, they will be ill-considered and have unanticipated consequences. The uncertainty suggests taking a balanced approach rather than relying exclusively on any one strategy. Having assets in all three types of accounts will help you fine-tune your taxes and your retirement income.

What Assets to Hold in Each Account?

Researchers find that people typically fill their taxable and tax-deferred accounts arbitrarily with the same assets. Individuals do this out of ignorance; investment advisors do it for convenience. Nevertheless, it is wrong. Bad dog!

Here are the guiding principles. The answer in one sentence is to put stocks in taxable accounts and bonds in tax-deferred accounts.

If your life-situation allows, *consider all your assets as part of one big happy household portfolio.* Then park each asset in whichever account is most advantageous, tax-wise.

If you do, some accounts will perform better than others, depending on how the assets they contain have done lately. This can be disconcerting. You see your IRA is up 3% when your brokerage account is up 10%, and think, gee, there's something wrong with my IRA. This is why investment companies set up every account with the same assets—so they don't have to deal with phone calls from clients wondering what is wrong with their

IRAs. But these differences are a good thing: they show that you have a diversified portfolio and that your tax alpha plan is working.

I am not going to address what your portfolio should look like—your asset *allocation*. That is for you and your advisors to thrash out. Here we are only concerned with the technical question of which asset goes where—your asset *location*.

Roth IRAs

If you have a Roth IRA/Roth 401(k), start here. Place the assets here that have the highest long-term expected return. More simply, stocks.

I also put moonshots here. Your crazy brother-in-law works for a startup. He can get you a hundred shares. There is a 99% chance they are worth zero and a 1% chance they are worth a million dollars. Put them in a Roth if you can.

Your Roth IRA is the first account to fill.

Tax-Deferred Accounts

In your IRA and 401(k), the asset of choice is taxable bonds or anything income-oriented, such as REITs or dividend stocks. Why? Because you avoid the annual hedge clipping that interest and coupons and dividends get from the government when they are held in taxable accounts.

Advisors used to put stocks in an IRA first, because of the tax-deferred compounding. This turned out to be a mistake. Capital appreciation inside an IRA converts capital gains into ordinary income, which is taxed at even higher rates, effectively transmuting gold into lead.

(Speaking of gold, bullion is taxed as a "collectible" at a high 28% capital gains rate, so there is an advantage to holding it inside an IRA as well.)

Then, on second look, advisors decided it was better to hold stocks outside of an IRA. This also turned out to be a mistake.

Why? Because once you add stock dividends and portfolio turnover to the mix, most stock mutual funds still perform better in an IRA over the long run. The expense of paying taxes at marginal rates upon withdrawal from the IRA adds up to less than the annual tax pruning for twenty to thirty years inside the taxable account, which nibbles away at your fortune like rats in a granary. Unless you are following a disciplined low-dividend, low-turnover strategy in your taxable accounts, most stock funds (other than stock market index funds) fare better in IRAs and 401(k)s over the long run.

Actively managed mutual funds belong in tax-deferred accounts because of their high internal turnover and the potential for non-qualified dividends. The same would hold for any "trading" accounts you manage. High turnover means high taxes. Picture a cow being lowered into a pool of piranhas, and you have it exactly.

Finally, bonds (except municipal bonds) belong inside traditional IRA/401(k) accounts. This goes double for Treasury inflation-protected bonds (TIPS) because they generate what is called "phantom" income. Phantom income is imputed income on which you must pay taxes even though you haven't been given the cash.

Taxable Accounts

Taxable accounts are the best place for securities that are going to appreciate but will not throw off more taxable income than you need to spend this year, briefly, individual stocks and index funds. The ideal holdings from a tax perspective would be numerous uncorrelated assets that you rarely trade. Second place goes to passive, market-wide exchange-traded index funds (ETFs). From there it is a steep, slippery slide into a tax abyss.

If you are primarily interested in the bequest angle, it will be better to leave the stocks in your taxable account instead of bloating your traditional IRA with them. Taxable accounts get a step up in basis; IRAs don't.

Specific Issues

Some assets fall through the cracks.

Funds versus Stocks

For maximum control of taxes and dividends, hold individual stocks in your taxable account, not funds. This is complete heresy to most investment advisors and a topic to which we will return with a vengeance later. For now, let's mention the downsides. Can you pick stocks? Probably not. Can you beat the market? As if! Can you deal with the *tracking error* of your handpicked stock portfolio—the fact that your account might be down 5% when the market is up 5%? I didn't think so.

Notwithstanding these objections, we will come to argue in favor of precisely this approach for people in high tax brackets. It is even more tax-efficient than holding a low-turnover index fund.

Traditional Mutual Funds

Even if you hold a mutual fund for a year without buying or selling a share, you will still have to pay taxes on it if it is held in a taxable account. All mutual funds are required to pay out all the dividends paid to the companies they hold along with the capital gains from their trading every year.

That said, some asset vehicles are inherently more tax-efficient than others. Always make the most tax-friendly choices in your taxable account.

Everything you have heard about how "passive" investing beats active management goes double after-tax. Passive investments such as an S&P 500 Index fund have very low portfolio turnover because managers are only buying and selling companies when stocks are voted in and out of the index. This low churn means they don't gin up much in the way of capital gains. You can check a mutual fund's turnover rate at Morningstar.com.

While you are there, drill down to Morningstar's "Tax Cost Ratio." This metric assumes you paid dividends and capital gains at the 15% rate. For a high earner, the rate might be twice as high (and don't forget state taxes), but it's still useful for making comparisons among funds. The lower the number, the less you sacrifice to taxes.

You can also lookup your fund's potential capital gains exposure at Morningstar.com under the "Price" tab. When you buy a traditional mutual fund, you expose yourself to the risk of getting your unfair share of this tax bill. People stampede for the exits during a panic, when the embedded gains may have already vanished to some extent. People who patiently hold on to a mutual fund during a year when it loses money are famously rewarded for their discipline with a fat year-end tax bill.

This year's hot mutual fund can disguise the effect of these gains because they get distributed over an expanding base of shareholders. Conversely, a shrinking fund (where investors are departing the burning building) leaves the realized gains to be divided by those left behind.

Traditional mutual funds sometimes come in "tax-managed" editions that try to cut the tax bill. They use several strategies: avoiding dividend-paying stocks, making sure they hold dividend stocks for over sixty days so that all dividends are taxed at the lower "qualified dividend" rate, keeping their turnover low, realizing capital gains losses aggressively, and trying to hold their winners for over one year before selling. While these efforts are all to the good, they can also handcuff the fund's investment strategy. Even if a mutual fund markets itself as "tax-managed," that doesn't mean you wouldn't be better off holding the same asset class in an ETF instead.

Exchange-Traded Funds

In the universe of passive index funds, there are still levels and levels. Exchange-traded funds (ETFs) run cooler than traditional mutual funds because the ETF structure allows them to swap out the stocks with capital gains in the course of creating and redeeming units without having actually to sell them. Exchange-traded funds also sidestep the problem of forcing you to pay taxes on capital gains run up by other investors, as with traditional mutual funds. Both traditional mutual funds and ETFs can and will have unrealized capital gains in the stocks they hold, but the traditional mutual funds cannot dissipate them along the way because they are not into "swapping." When capital gains are realized, it will be on your timetable, not the fund's.

This is an unfair advantage for ETFs. Note carefully, tax alpha dogs! The only exception to this rule is at Vanguard, where their stock index mutual funds have a patent to shift out their gains through the ETF classes of the same funds.

"Factor" Investing

Academics have analyzed long-term stock market performance and statistically determined which factors explain the returns. Then they design mutual funds to capture these effects. As Columbia's Andrew Ang says, "factors are to assets as nutrients are to food."

Table 2.3 shows how various factor approaches compare to the benchmark Vanguard Total U.S. Stock Market Index Fund. The data are from Morningstar, and here bigger is worse: this is how much your annual investment returns would have been diminished by taxes, assuming a dividend and capital gains rate of 15% (and in reality, yours might be over twice that high, Federal and state).

TABLE 2.2 Factor fund tax efficiency			
Factor	Ticker	1-year tax cost	3-year tax cost
Benchmark: U.S. stock index	VTI	0.78%	0.57%
Small/value stocks	PRFZ	0.50%	0.37%
Momentum stocks	MTUM	0.28%	0.30%
Low-volatility stocks	USMV	0.52%	0.53%

Any given time period might offer a very different picture. It does suggest that long-only factor investing can be compatible with tax efficiency. Mutual fund companies that sell factor-style products believe that their outperformance will surpass their tax liabilities relative to the market wide index funds.

Taxable versus Municipal Bonds

A significant fudge factor is that you can use municipal bonds as a release valve when you need to park your bond allocation inside your taxable account. There are calculators all over the Internet that will tell you whether taxable or muni bonds pay a higher yield after-tax in your bracket. If you live in a high-tax state, keep in mind that U.S. Treasury bonds are not taxable at the state level. Use these calculators to determine which kind of money market fund (taxable or muni) to hold in your taxable account as well.

Alternative Investments

Alternative investments typically generate short-term capital gains due to the high turnover of their underlying strategies. Furthermore, "short" sales (betting that a stock will go down) are always taxed at high short-term rates because short selling is considered un-American. So are the gains from trading options, another alternative specialty.

The "liquid alternatives" mutual funds are excellent candidates for your IRA, as are other potentially tax-intensive assets such as hedge funds and private equity. Unfortunately, the name-brand IRA custodians won't accept these latter investments. You'll have to set up a "self-directed IRA" at a small shop specializing in them.

Do not put anything into an IRA if it generates what is called "unrelated business tax income" such as Master Limited Partnerships. The IRA chassis offers no protection in this instance, and your IRA could end up having to file a tax return (both Federal and in the states where the income originates), which takes the fun out of it.

Foreign Stocks

Foreign stocks are tricky because they pay high dividends, but your taxes depend on whether the country has a tax treaty with us. Their dividends are taxed and withheld in the country of origin. Then, to give you a kick in the pants, the IRS taxes you on your foreign income regardless of whether it was already taxed abroad.

To make it up to you, the IRS offers a credit for the foreign taxes you have paid. You have to fill out Form 1116 to get it, which is another bag of snakes (but Turbo Tax Premier reputedly can handle it). For foreign partnerships, tax reporting alone can cost thousands of dollars.

You can duck this problem by keeping foreign stocks in your IRA. That way you are not taxed on the dividends at all, but at the significant price of forgoing any credit for the taxes you paid to the foreign countries.

The preferred asset location for foreign stocks depends entirely upon the specifics of your tax situation. There is no general answer or reliable rule of thumb.

REITs

Real Estate Investment Trusts have benefited from the TCJA because 20% of their income is sheltered from federal taxes.

However, this means 80% still is not. It remains advantageous to park them in tax-deferred accounts.

A First Pass at Tax Alpha Asset Location

You have a bunch of different accounts—what do you put where?

You open the box and shake the pieces onto the floor. Then you try to put each investment where it will do the least harm, tax-wise. Your asset allocation won't divide perfectly into the three account types because you don't have unlimited headroom in each one. You may have to shoehorn some investment somewhere it may not belong. Or you may already have a lot of embedded capital gains and can't move them assets without triggering them.

Table 2.3 gives you the cheat sheet.

Keep in mind that if you are going to be periodically rebalancing your accounts, it is helpful to have both stocks and bonds in your tax-deferred accounts so that you can rebalance between them without incurring a tax liability.

The Boneyard

🦴 Register your taxable accounts in a way that fits your situation.

🦴 Name people as primary and secondary beneficiaries of your IRAs if you don't have a retirement trust that can stretch the payouts. If you do name a retirement trust as the beneficiary, this may be DOA if the Secure Act has passed.

🦴 Select the automated cost basis reporting that makes the best tax choices for you in your taxable accounts.

TABLE 2.3 Which asset goes where?
Roth accounts
Moonshots
Small/value stock funds
Momentum funds
Tax-deferred accounts
Taxable bonds
REITs
Most alternative investments
Gold
Dividend stocks
Low-volatility stock funds
Actively managed stock funds
Taxable accounts
Zero/low dividend stocks
Stock index exchange-traded funds
M.L.P.s
Municipal bonds
Cash

- In general, fund tax-sheltered accounts to the limit every year.
- If your taxes will be lower after you retire than they are today, go traditional IRA/401(k); if they will be higher after you retire, go Roth.
- Place highly taxed assets such as bonds in tax-deferred accounts.
- Avoid mutual funds with a high internal turnover in your taxable accounts unless you are in the lowest tax bracket, and then avoid them anyway. Use passive market-wide index funds instead.
- Prefer exchange-traded funds over ordinary mutual funds in your taxable accounts
- Manage your accounts on a "household" basis (where you think of your family's accounts as one overall portfolio), so you can position each asset in the right account for maximum tax advantage.

Chapter Three

Tax Tricks **for Treats**

*Any one may so arrange his affairs that his taxes shall
be as low as possible; he is not bound to choose that
pattern which will best pay the Treasury; there is not
even a patriotic duty to increase one's taxes.*

—Learned Hand

Do you believe that people should pay more taxes than legally required? I have good news. The Treasury Department accepts "Gifts to the United States" at P.O. Box 1328, Parkersburg, W. Virginia 26106. Make your check payable to "U.S. Treasury." Thank you for your contribution.

Most taxpayers, however, prefer to pay only their minimum annual requirement. In this chapter, we will review various legal means people routinely use to minimize their tax bills. Some of these items will be relevant to you; many will not. If a particular strategy is not a fit, skip it.

Let me start with this gem from CPA Robert Keebler. When researching the estate tax, Keebler stumbled upon the fact that *every client of his who had an estate tax problem had gotten there by maximizing the use of statutory tax shelters.*

In this context, having an estate tax problem was a *good* thing: it meant that the client had too much money. Keebler's point, worth knitting into a sampler and hanging above your fireplace, is that it is almost impossible to get rich if you hand over half your earnings to the government every year. The government's share is probably more than half once you add in your various other taxes. If your wealth consists of a big salary, you will be a wage slave who drives a Mercedes. Real wealth comes from following a more efficient tax path.

Accounts that are Statutory Tax Shelters

Traditional Retirement Accounts

Retirement accounts are the premier statutory tax shelters. The money you contribute gives you a tax write-off, and then your money escapes taxes on capital gains, dividends and interest while it compounds year after year.

In most cases, you have until April 15 of the following year to open and fund your retirement accounts, but the smart move is to fund them as soon as you can. Table 3.1 shows the contribution limits. These limits are subject to conditions, but this is the ballpark.

TABLE 3.1 Plan Contribution Limits 2020				
Age	IRA and Roth	SEP IRA	SIMPLE IRA	401(k)
Under 50	$6,000	$57,000	$13,500	$19,500
50 and older	$7,000	$57,000	$16,500	$26,000

Solo 401(k)

If you are self-employed, set up a Solo 401(k) in preference to a SEP IRA or a SIMPLE IRA. The Solo 401(k) takes more paperwork, and you will reach a point where you must mail in Form 5500 in July every year, but once these niceties are taken care of, you will be better off. These plans let you shelter more money from taxes at lower income levels (up to $63,500 annually for those aged fifty and older). You can also hire an administrator to set up a Solo Roth 401(k) for after-tax contributions, and you can do "backdoor Roth" conversions (see below).

Defined Benefit Plans

These plans are for high-earning, older professionals or small business owners who are either sole proprietors or who have a small number of much lower compensated employees. These plans also work for anyone with a W-2 who has a side hustle that produces reliable income not needed for current consumption.

You need enough disposable business income to fund the plan annually. This is additional money you want to set aside after funding your other retirement accounts. The money doesn't have to come from your business, and the older you are, the more you can contribute.

First, you hire an actuary to set up and administer the plan. The actuary tailors the plan to your circumstances, and you will have to make a fixed annual tax-deductible contribution to it. If you contribute $100,000, your business earns $100,000 less that year. Set up the account with a custodian of your choice. You control the investments. Invest in something relatively stable (bonds?) to avoid issues with under- or overfunding the plan.

There will be an annual fee to the plan administrator for the ongoing actuarial calculation to ensure the account is funded on schedule. The plan has to include all employees who meet the criteria for inclusion, but you can arrange for the lion's share goes to you. There is also a ticking clock attached—the plan closes in five or seven or ten years, or whenever you decide.

At that point, you can roll the plan over into an IRA. Instead of saving $6,000 annually with a traditional IRA, a defined benefit plan will let you bank six-figure sums—on top of whatever you put into your other retirement accounts.

What if you shutter the business? What if you can't come up with the money? Does that put you in the soup? No, you close the plan. Notify the IRS and roll the money into an IRA. What if you decide not to retire? You amend the plan. As you can see, these plans are flexible. If you qualify and you can afford to fund one, it pays to defer taxes, unless you anticipate being in a higher bracket in retirement than you are today.

Roth and Roth Conversions

There is a lot to love about Roth IRAs:

- tax-free compounding
- no mandatory distributions during your (or your spouse's) lifetime
- no taxes on distributions from the plan after five years or age $59\frac{1}{2}$
- lifetime distribution for non-spouse heirs under present law, or at least ten years of continued tax postponement if the Secure Act passes

- withdrawals during retirement can be used to fine-tune your tax bracket
- withdrawals during retirement do not affect how your Social Security or Medicare will be taxed

Roths have the same low contribution limits as traditional IRAs. Furthermore, there are income limits to participating: contributions are curtailed above a modified adjusted income of $124,000 for single/$196,000 for married and are phased out altogether soon after that. This makes it hard for the very-high-income to build sizeable Roth accounts following conventional methods.

There are no income limits on contributing to a Roth 401(k) through your employer plan if it offers one. The contribution limits are $19,500 per year in 2020 ($26,000 if you are fifty or older). But if the plan allows, workers can contribute to an after-tax 401(k) up to a total all-in contribution limit of $57,000 ($63,500 catch-up for those fifty and over). Some plans allow in-plan conversions or rollovers to Roth IRAs, which should be done immediately so that the future growth will be tax-free. Otherwise, when you punch out from your job, roll the after-tax portion to a Roth IRA. This is the best Roth deal that high earners are going to see.

The other way to put a foot-long hot dog inside the Roth bun is by converting your traditional IRA to a Roth. You pay the taxes at your marginal rate that year on the sum you convert. Should you proceed?

Roth conversions make the most sense when you can do them cheaply. A good year would be when you have net operating losses, offsetting charitable contributions, investment tax credits, or deductions greater than your income. Did your husband break his leg on the ski slope and require a helicopter MedEvac followed by multiple, expensive surgeries? Look at the bright side: this may present an opportunity to do a Roth conversion.

Once your required minimum IRA distributions (RMDs) begin, they increase every year, at least as a percentage of your remaining account. A Roth conversion today can keep you from trespassing into a higher tax bracket later. If strategic Roth conversions mean you can stay in a lower bracket throughout retirement, they can still be cost-effective even after the up-front tax bite. But do the math first. More on this later.

Pay the taxes for the conversion from sources outside the IRA, to keep as much money as possible inside the Roth wrapper. If this entails realizing a lot of capital gains in your taxable account to raise the cash to pay the tax bill, that makes the conversion less efficient.

Roth conversions need to be done carefully because under TCJA they can no longer be re-characterized if you change your mind later. Follow the advice of Davy Crockett: "Be sure you're right—then go ahead."

RMDs are always the first money out of your IRA. Take your entire RMD, and then do your Roth conversion. There is no need to convert every penny of the traditional IRA. Keep some money in there for tax risk diversification. You can always use it for charitable giving or to fill you lower tax bracket sleeves, or you can convert it later, perhaps in a year of high medical expenses.

Backdoor Roth Conversions

Strangely, the government imposes income limits on Roth contributions but not on Roth conversions. This pointless distinction creates the "backdoor Roth" strategy for people whose incomes are too high to allow them to fund a Roth directly. Once controversial, the "backdoor" Roth is now accepted by the IRS.

Open a traditional nondeductible IRA and put $6,000 of post-tax earned income into it ($7,000 if you are fifty or older). Then convert this to a Roth IRA, tax-free. While not a tremendous sum of money, if done year after year, the amount can become meaningful over time.

The hitch is the *pro rata rule*, which requires you to consider the value of all your IRAs when paying taxes on the conversion. If you already have $95,000 in a traditional IRA and convert a $5,000 post-tax IRA to a Roth, the conversion will be 95% taxable. A workaround might be to do a "roll-in" to shuttle your pretax IRA into your 401(k) plan (including a solo 401(k) plan, if the plan sponsor will let you), which is not counted in the *pro rata* calculation.

Finally, you file Form 8606 with your taxes, notifying the IRS about your nondeductible IRA contribution.

A working stiff can also do this for a non-working spouse, culminating in the "backdoor spouse" Roth maneuver.

Custodial Roths

Roths are super-valuable for your kids. If your child has beavered away at a summer job, match whatever she earned (up to $6,000 in 2020) and park this amount in a custodial Roth IRA. If you can sock away $6,000 for four years, and it compounds at 6% annually until she retires at age seventy, that would leave her with half a million dollars, tax-free. Not a bad way to begin retirement.

Depending on the age of majority in your state, the account needs to be rolled over to a regular Roth IRA when she turns eighteen. At that point, the account is hers. She can pull the money outright then if she's willing to pay the penalties. If she uses it to run off with a motorcycle gang, this could prove to be a mistake.

Roths and Estate Planning

If the Secure Act has passed, Roth IRAs have become much less valuable for estate planning, but they still have some value. The ideal would be to hold the Roth untouched through your lifetime and that of your surviving spouse, and then have it go to your kids for the final ten years of compounding inside the Roth wrapper before they have to pull all the money out at the end of year ten.

Recall that Roths make the most sense when your taxes today are lower than your taxes tomorrow. This same seesaw principle applies across generations. Compare your children's marginal tax rates to yours. If theirs are higher, bequeathing Roth IRAs makes sense (converting your Traditional IRAs to Roths for the kids at your lower tax rates). But if your kids' taxes are lower than yours, leave them your traditional IRAs and let them pay the taxes.

If you end up with one kid who is a hedge fund manager while the other does missionary work in the Congo, leave the hedgie your Roth and leave the missionary your traditional IRA, making allowance for the difference in the after-tax value of the two bequests. A Roth is always worth 100 cents on the dollar, whereas a traditional IRA is worth 100 cents minus the kid's marginal tax rate.

The other estate-planning angle of a Roth conversion is that the money you pay in taxes doing the conversion during your lifetime is out of your estate. If the estate tax is going to be an issue for you, do a total Roth conversion and pay the taxes now—otherwise your estate will pay taxes on money that will be taxed again when pulled out from an inherited traditional IRA. Your heirs can get a tax credit for this, but they may or may not be made whole even if they claim and apply it correctly, which rarely happens.

Retirement Accounts—Closing Thoughts

The benefit to you of investing in any retirement account—beyond claiming an employer match, which is an instantaneous 100% return—entirely depends on the arbitrage from the taxes you save by putting the money into the accounts today versus the taxes you pay when you (or your surviving spouse or your heirs) pull the money out later. If taxes today and more than taxes later, you are better off in a Traditional IRA. If taxes today are less than taxes later, you are better off in a Roth. A taxable investment account can work nearly as well as a Roth if you use it to best advantage, buying and holding super-low dividend stocks and never trading the account except to harvest tax losses.

Whether the Secure Act passed this time around or not, those who have not yet begun taking required minimum distributions should consider how big to let their pre-tax accounts grow. There is a considerable political risk that we might be force-fed larger distributions whether we want them or not. A defensive rule of thumb would be not to let the tax-deferred accounts grow to a size where you would not be comfortable taking the entire amount as a distribution within your lifetime. This is the direction that our annuity-happy Congress is pushing us. If the inflated RMDs would scaffold you into a Federal bracket ten percentage points higher than the one you would otherwise be paying, it might be time to cap this gusher, forgo the tax deduction today, and park your money in a Roth or a taxable account instead.

Health Savings Accounts

Health Savings Accounts (HSAs) are only allowed for people with high-deductible health insurance plans ($1,400 individuals/$2,800 families in 2020). The idea is to help them meet medical expenses by giving them a triple tax-free vehicle: tax-deductible savings, tax-free growth, and tax-free withdrawals. Contribution limits are $3,550 individuals/$7,100 families in 2020, with an extra $1,000 catch-up contribution for people aged fifty-five and older. Sometimes there is even an employer match.

These accounts are much too valuable to waste buying Axe body spray and Flintstone vitamins. The smart use of an HSA is to invest the money in the stock market and let the savings compound tax-deferred. Then take the money out to pay for the large and growing list of medical expenses not covered by Medicare during retirement (hearing, vision, dental, to name three). A retired couple is projected to spend between $280,000 and $320,000 on non-reimbursed medical expenses, much of it late in life. Whatever the figure is, it won't be small. Set up an HSA when you are young and leaving it alone to compound for decades. You can leave anything left over to your spouse, but non-spouse heirs lose all the HSA tax advantages. They have to claim the HSA balance as ordinary income the year they get it, and there is no deduction for using it for medical expenses.

529 Plans

Once Junior gets that acceptance letter, he needs more than a Stutz Bearcat, a raccoon coat, a ukulele, and a hip flask. He needs money for tuition and room and board. That's where the 529 plan comes in. These are investment accounts specifically designed to encourage saving for college. If you will be paying for your child's college expenses, start putting the money in a 529 plan the day the kid is conceived (you can do it that early) and stick on the social security number nine months later.

How much will you need? Use the Sallie Mae college cost calculator to find out. Trigger warning: make sure you are in a safe space with a bottle of smelling salts nearby when you look at the result.

https://www.salliemae.com/college-planning/tools/college-cost-calculator/

The TCJA has expanded 529 plans to cover private elementary and high schools. Because the accounts allow tax-free compounding of returns, the best strategy is to invest as much as you can as early as you can and let the growth pay for college.

The long-term compounding means that the accounts are most valuable when used for college (or graduate school), less valuable for high school, still less valuable for elementary school, and have the least value to add to kindergarten, where you might only capture five years of investment growth. Your home state might also tax you on K-12 distributions, even though the Feds do not.

After-tax contributions are made using your $15,000 (per parent) annual gift exclusion. Gifts can be front-loaded (up to five years' worth during the first year, or $150,000 for a couple donating to one child). If you make this 5-year election, either individually or as a split gift, you must so report it that year on Form 709, the Federal gift tax return. If you can afford it, the best approach is to fund the plan with $15,000 from each parent when the child is conceived and then, after January 1 ticks by, superfund the plan with five years' worth of contributions.

The savings compound tax-free, and distributions are again tax-free when used for qualified higher educational expenses (tuition, room and board, textbooks, computers). Some wealthy parents will pay the tuition separately since the tax code lets them without using their annual $15,000 gift tax exclusion, and then use the 529 plan to pay for the other educational expenses. This transfers more wealth to the child. Very wealthy parents may use 529 plans inside a Dynasty Trust to secure multi-generational educational funding for their offspring.

Investigate the pros and cons of your own state's plan just as a point of reference. Nearly every state offers a 529 plan—some are much better than others—and you can use any state's plan you want. A student can be a beneficiary of more than one state's plan. My current favorites are states that offer flexible plans with high contribution limits and Vanguard funds: New York, Ohio, Pennsylvania, and Utah.

Some states allow you to take a state tax deduction for your contribution. I have heard of cases where parents contribute to their home state's mediocre, expensive plan just to collect the deduction, and then discreetly moved the money to a better out-of-state plan later. In some cases, the state left behind might consider this rollover to be a non-qualified distribution for state income tax purposes—either the entire amount or for the initial amount invested. On the other hand, residents of six states (Arizona, Kansas, Minnesota, Missouri, Montana, and Pennsylvania) can take the tax deduction even if you use a different state's plan. If you weigh the benefits of the tax deduction by spreading out the contributions over eighteen years versus superfunding the plan from year zero, the latter strategy is likely to transfer more net worth.

If you work in a high-liability field, you should also investigate the creditor protections available to the plan, which also vary by state. If you are in a risky business, your spouse or your sister might be a better owner.

The money in the plan belongs to you, not your kid. You can change the beneficiaries to other family members and roll the plans over to other states, but moving the beneficiary down a generation may use part of your generation-skipping tax exemption if you don't do it in $75,000-per-five-year install-ments. There is a 10% penalty on top of ordinary income taxes (at the beneficiary's tax rate) on any earnings distributed for non-educational use.

I have heard of cases where family members or friends make cross-gifts to the 529 plans of each other's children, inflating the contributions. The Court of Appeals ruled in one case that same-day reciprocal gifts to each other's children were actually intended to benefit the taxpayer's own children (!) and so the gift tax applied.

If you apply for financial aid and have UTMA/UGMA accounts, the college will expect 20% of the value of these accounts to be part of the expected family contribution. The college will also expect to take 20% of any savings directly in the student's name. On the other hand, only 5.64% of the balance of the 529 plans is expected to be part of the family contribution.

You can pare this further if you keep two 529 plans in Grandpa and Grandma's name (so it is not listed as a parental or child asset by the college), and then use these accounts to pay for the child's junior and senior years. Unlike with the parent's plan, this disbursement would have to be reported as income on the FAFSA form by the student, but since FAFSA has a two-year lookback you would be safe.

But – if the student is going to seek financial aid for graduate school, the junior and senior year 529 plan income from Grandpa and Grandma will show up on his or her tax records. In that case, it would be better for Mom and Dad to pay for everything from their 529 plan. Parental assets are usually not evaluated for graduate school financial aid since by then the student is considered an adult. Back on the farm, Grandpa and Grandma could transfer $15,000 each from their 529 plans to the 529 plan run by their adult child (the college kid's parent), and that money could be used to help pay for both college and graduate school while keeping the parent's 529 plan balance as low as possible. The grandparents can make only one transfer per 12-month period, or it violates the $15,000-per-year rule. In balancing the plans, do whatever is least harmful to the financial aid package: counting 5.64% of the parent's 529 plan balance, versus counting 50% of the grandparent's 529 plan payout to the grandchild.

What is the alternative? Keep the money in your brokerage account, pay taxes on the distributions year after year, and then get hit with capital gains taxes when you sell your stocks to pay tuition? These are taxes paid for no reason.

For kids in graduate school, remember that once they are over age 24, they have escaped the clutches of the "kiddie tax." Anyone can gift them $15,000 worth of appreciated securities every year, which they can sell to fund their education and likely pay 0% capital gains tax. This makes more sense than selling the stocks, paying 23.8% (+ state taxes) on the capital gains, and then using the money left over to pay tuition.

529 plans also have off-label uses in estate planning to move assets out of the estate. In the wake of the overall devaluation of retirement plans threatened by the Secure Act, overfunding 529 plans might be a viable alternative. The amount not spent on college continues to compound inside the plan, and when the grandchild is born the child uses the gift tax exclusion in five-year increments to transfer his plan's assets to the grand-child's plan until the old plan is emptied. If no bright and shiny college kids come your way, you can always use the money to fund your own educational opportunities in later life—perhaps at golf school in Hilton Head, film school in London, art school in Glasgow, or culinary classes in New York.

Statutory Tax Shelters inside Taxable Accounts

Capital Gains

A capital gain (or loss) is the difference between the amount you paid for something (its "basis") and the amount you earned upon its sale. Taxing people on their capital gains is notoriously a second tax on corporate profits, which were already taxed at the corporate level. It also encompasses a tax on inflation. In some cases, the only capital gains you receive will be inflation, and you will be taxed on them anyway. Inflation is a tax created by the Federal Reserve's failure to maintain price stability. Thus, capital gains are triple-taxed.

Nevertheless, there is something to love about capital gains. You pay no tax until you sell the security. The tax rates are usually lower than the tax rates for ordinary income. Finally, the nominal capital gains rates overstate your actual liability, since you might be paying a 15% tax in the future on capital gains deferred for decades.

Here's the kicker: your heirs get a cost basis reset to fair market value when you exit the terrestrial plane, which means the capital gains might never be taxed at all.

All this makes capital gains the premier statutory tax shelter, as they have been since the Revenue Act of 1921. They are the last best tax break for the middle class, but don't worry—the upper class finds them useful as well.

University of Chicago professor George Constantinides figured out the best tactic for capital gains in 1983: "The optimal liquidation policy is to *realize losses immediately and defer gains* until the event of a forced liquidation." In other words, as economist David

Ricardo advised two hundred years ago, cut short your losses and let your winners run on. Most investors do the opposite: they realize gains and avoid realizing losses because this preserves the comforting illusion that someday they will be made whole.

Capital gains (or losses) fall into two categories, depending on how long you own the asset: short term or long term.

A short-term gain (or loss) occurs when you hold an asset one year or less. Realized short-term gains can be painful because they are taxed at your marginal tax rate as ordinary income or possibly even higher if the 3.8% Obamacare surtax applies (although your ordinary income would likely be subject to the 2.9% Medicare tax and the 0.9% supplemental Medicare tax, so there may not be a tremendous difference).

Long-term gains (or losses) occur on assets held more than one year. Note carefully, tax alpha dog: if you place an order for a mutual fund on January 1 this year and sell it January 1 next year, it's still a short-term gain—because your holding period is not *over* one year.

The capital gains brackets are supposed to line up with the income tax brackets, but in the breathless rush to pass the TCJA, nobody bothered to align them.

Table 3.2 shows the long-term capital gains tax rates according to your tax bracket.

TABLE 3.2 Capital gains tax rates by adjusted gross income, 2020			
Individual	Married	Long-term rate	+ Obamacare
< $40,000	< $80,000	0%	0%
to $200,000	to $250,000	15%	0%
to $441,450	to $496,600	15%	3.80%
> $441,450	> $496,600	20%	3.80%

If you are single and have no income, that does not mean that you can raise a million dollars of capital gains that year and pay no taxes. Au contraire, once they cross the thresholds above, they will be taxed at progressive capital gains rates: The first $40,000 will be tax-free, the next chunk up to $200,000 will be taxed at 15%, then the next bite up to $441,450 will be taxed at 18.3%, and any remainder will be taxed at 23.8%. Of course, because of deductions, you wouldn't owe any tax until you realized gains amounting to $52,400 (single) or $104,800 (married), assuming no other income. State taxes will be on top of these. Taxpayers over 65 are allowed an additional $1,350 deduction apiece.

Unfortunately, in determining which bracket your capital gains fall in, capital gains stack on top of ordinary income. Ordinary income swings both ways because it fills your lower capital gains buckets. It tops off the 0% capital gains bracket shown in Table 3.2, crowding out investors' precious 0% capital gains tax rate opportunity. Once you stir in ordinary income, more of your capital gains (and dividends) are taxed at higher rates. More on this later.

A few other points:

- For stocks that pay dividends in the form of shares instead of cash, these new shares will have the same short- or long-term status as the underlying stock. The dividends will be taxed as capital gains when the stock is sold.
- Short sellers (people who borrow shares and sell them, hoping that the stock price will go down before they have to rebuy them) always pay short-term capital gains rates, regardless of the holding period.
- Inherited stock always has a long-term cost basis, no matter when the stock was acquired.
- Depreciation recapture on investment real estate is taxed at 25% (section 1250 gains).
- Long-term collectibles (including precious metals) are taxed at 28%.

Every year, you report your gains and losses in each of these categories to the IRS, broken down by holding period. The short-term gains and losses are added up, and so are the long-term gains and losses. Then the two are "netted" against each other in a nettlesome process. Fortunately, your brokerage will sort all this out for you on your year-end tax statement.

As noted, exchange-traded funds (ETFs) avoid the accelerated capital gains distributions that regular mutual funds pass out. Individual stocks do not generate capital gains or losses until sold, giving you maximum control over the timing of the recognition of capital gains.

When gains must be realized, sell the shares that you have held longer than one year with the highest cost basis. This is where the brokerage account settings mentioned in the previous chapter come into play. If possible, realize capital gains during a year when you are in a low tax bracket.

Taxes add to the cost of changing investment strategies. Advisors relish gleefully selling everything to move a client into their new space-age model. But the tax paid in consequence is money gone forever. The new strategy not only needs to make a better return than the old one but must overcome this self-created tax hurdle to get back to the starting line. Be judicious when switching strategies.

Capital Gains When Rebalancing Your Portfolio

Taxes also add to the cost of rebalancing. Although postponing gains and realizing losses is the optimal tax strategy, it is not optimal for everyone. Many investors practice portfolio rebalancing, selling outperformers and buying laggards to preserve a set stock/bond allocation. Most of the time, this means selling stocks to buy bonds.

People in low brackets can rebalance without tax consequences. People in high brackets often live with high allocations to stocks in their taxable accounts, where rebalancing, if done at all, needs to be practiced with extreme circumspection because the gains realized from the attendant sales will be highly taxed. Investors in the middle brackets with both taxable and tax-qualified accounts should weigh the trade-off between the benefits from rebalancing, which are hypothetical, vs. the costs, which are certain. A few workarounds:

- Try to do as much of the rebalancing as possible inside tax-deferred accounts, such as your 401(k).
- Only rebalance to the nearest edge of your rebalancing tolerance band. Don't go all the way.
- Rebalance at the "asset class" level, that is, stocks to bonds. Don't rebalance at the "sub-asset class" level, for example, U.S. mid-cap value stocks to U.S. mid-cap growth stocks. These are angels dancing on the head of a pin. Rebalancing to some arbitrary fixed division between them will have no foreseeable risk impact.

- Rebalance using new money, including the cash distributions from existing assets (rather than having your distributions reinvested automatically).
- Sell your highest-cost shares first.

As with so many questions in life, this a question not of how but of how many. Let's put some numbers to it to see the kind of rebalancing cost-benefit analysis you should perform. Imagine that you hold $1,000,000 targeted to a vintage 60/40 stock/bond portfolio. Your money is divided between index funds representing the total U.S. stock market and the total U.S. bond market.

Next, as a result of market action, your portfolio grows to 65% stocks/35% bonds. What are the costs and benefits of rebalancing back to 60/40? According to my Quantext Monte Carlo analysis (using round numbers):

- At 65/35, you would make $88,000 in a median year, but you could lose $143,000 in the worst 1% of years.
- Back in 60/40 land, you would make $85,000 in a median year, but you might lose $130,000 in the worst 1% of years.

If one-third of your stock allocation consists of capital gains, and you are a high earner who pays 28.6% federal + state taxes on your capital gains, the tax cost of rebalancing from 65/35 back to 60/40 inside a taxable account is roughly $5,000. Table 3.3 lays it out.

	Median gain	One percentile loss	Taxes
60/40	$85,000	($130,000)	–
65/35	$88,000	($143,000)	–
Rebalance	($3,000)	$13,000	($5,000)

TABLE 3.3
Portfolio rebalancing costs versus benefits

Would you pay $5,000 to avoid a 1% chance of losing $13,000, especially if it meant forgoing an additional $3,000 in expected returns? Probably not; it doesn't pencil out as an attractive bet.

Your numbers will be different. This is the kind of analysis that should be done before charging ahead. I am not dog-matically anti-rebalancing. My point is that it should be practiced with a cosmic consciousness of its costs and benefits and not done by rote. Rebalancing to control risk is most important to those on the cusp of retirement. Sharp early losses can adversely impact long-term retiree portfolio withdrawal survivability. For others, maybe the best course would be to tread lightly.

Capital Gains Fair Market Value Reset

Behold an idea of great beauty:

When you die with unrealized capital gains in your portfolio, your heirs get an immediate reset in their cost basis to that day's price (or, if they prefer, the price six months later). They can't cherry-pick: they must value the entire estate on one of those two dates.

This is not because of the government's generosity. It's because you are dead, so there's nothing more they can do to compel you to tell them what you paid for everything.

The way your assets are titled affects this process. Sole property gets a step-up. Community property gets a step-up even if only one spouse dies. Joint tenancy only gets a step-up on the deceased partner's share.

This reset to fair market value is the centerpiece of estate planning. Used correctly, it allows you to leave your heirs the assets with the most value and optimize your tax bill across generations.

Capital Gains Distribution Avoidance

Toward year-end, mutual funds pay out the dividends and realized capital gains they have accumulated during the year, and exchange-traded funds pay out dividends. The fund families can give you a heads-up what's coming, and there's a website that will let you search for upcoming distributions using the fund's ticker.

http://www.capitalgainsvalet.com

The easiest way to avoid unwanted capital gains is by not buying a mutual fund right before it makes a year-end capital gains distribution.

Naturally, you will use low-turnover exchange-traded index funds or individual stocks where possible in taxable accounts. ETFs rarely make capital gains distributions, although the dividend and interest income payout will remain.

What about the funds you already own? Imagine that you cast your searchlight at the upcoming distributions and spot some bunker busters dropping into your taxable account in December. What can you do?

In theory, you could sell the fund before the record date. A "record date" is not when you go to the sock hop at the malt shop for a soda pop by the jukebox. It is, rather, the date on which all shareholders of record are selected to receive the forthcoming distribution. By selling the fund before this date, you are saying, "Include me out."

But—if you sell the fund before the record date, you have two problems. First, you may realize a capital gain that will be greater than the dividend you ducked. Second, if you realize a loss, you need to stay out of this fund for thirty-one days to avoid a disqualifying *wash sale* (to be explained shortly).

By combing through your share lots, you might be able to sell part of your position at breakeven and avoid some of the distribution. You still need to find a replacement fund, but it could be worth the effort.

Capital gains distribution avoidance is a trick for the more advanced tax alpha dogs. You can have a reasonably fulfilling life even without it.

To kill two birds with one stone, do year-end tax-loss harvesting before your mutual funds make their annual capital gains distributions.

Tax-Loss Harvesting

Tax-loss harvesting is the practice of deliberately selling losing positions to rake in a tax loss on the capital gains (which amount to capital losses at that point).

It is a great technique to offset realized capital gains elsewhere or just to knock $3,000 from your taxable income. Some experts think it can add 1.5% of alpha annually to an actively managed account and roughly 0.6% of tax alpha to a portfolio of index funds. It is a hobby worth pursuing.

Here is the decisive question: what are you going to do with the proceeds from the sale? If you rebuy the security immediately, or even within thirty days, this is a wash sale, which means the government is going to disallow it and wash that loss right out of your hair. Get the picture? This holds even if you sell it in your brokerage account and buy it in your IRA, or (if you file a joint tax return) buy it in your spouse's account. The IRS will disallow the loss.

Because you can't just buy back the security immediately, what are you going to use in its place? If you stay in cash waiting to re-buy it thirty-one days later, the stock will rocket up, and you will kick yourself for having sold it. Conversely, if you continue to hold the stock, it will fall like an anvil. This is one of the immutable laws of the stock market.

The answer is to buy something that will perform similarly, so you don't miss out on the fun. If you buy something "substantially identical,"—a term nowhere defined—the IRS will also disallow the loss, and it will be a wash sale. For example, if you sell one S&P 500 Index fund to claim a loss and then buy another S&P 500 Index fund from a different fund family, the IRS might argue that this is a distinction without a difference. However, by being clever, you can usually have your loss and eat it, too. For example, to my way of thinking, a total stock market index fund would behave similarly to an S&P 500 Index fund of only the five hundred largest stocks in the U.S. economy. I would look for a security where the performance is likely to be close to that of the original holding, but with some significant difference to talk up if necessary.

Do not buy anything as a replacement that you would not be tickled to own as a long-term holding in your portfolio.

While people usually harvest tax losses at the end of the year (if they bother to harvest them at all), ideally they reap the losses whenever they appear. Diligent tax alpha dogs periodically dig through shares of their holdings looking for the odd lot with a loss. Your account statement usually just displays the totals, and a total gain may disguise the fact that some of the underlying shares are available for harvesting.

The best use of short-term losses is to offset short-term gains or ordinary income because these are taxed at the highest rates. It is less valuable to use them to offset long-term losses, but any deduction is better than none.

Some people have large accumulations of tax losses. Taking a $3,000 deduction every year can require decades to work through them all. They are a wasting asset. Every year they sit on your shelf, they are free money loaned to the government, plus they get dinged by inflation. It's generally better to use them as we go along rather than saving them for the future. Our tax rate in retirement may be lower than it is today, so it pays to burn through them now. Even so, having a large chunk of capital losses is almost like owning another asset class—one that can allow you to take ongoing tax-free distributions from your brokerage account during retirement.

Tax-loss harvesting only postpones taxes. We book a loss today, but at the price of possibly having to pay a higher tax tomorrow. Does this make sense? Yes, because of the time value of money. The exception would be if the lower cost basis forces you into a higher bracket when you sell the stock later. But tomorrow may never come if you postpone realizing the gain long enough.

When you are on your death bed, your first call should be to your advisor, with instructions to sell every position registering a tax loss. Once you go to heaven, those losses are useless to anyone. Rage, rage against the dying of the light—at least until your advisor confirms they have been sold.

Here is a heartwarming story from attorney Carol Harrington to inspire us all.

A client's son called her firm one morning to report that his father had died at home that very day before the last set of trades scheduled for his portfolio were placed. Now the son was grieving not only at the death of his father but at the unnecessary taxes he would have to pay on his father's final tax return.

The quick-thinking attorney (Fred Ackers) told the young man, "You're not a doctor! Call an ambulance!"

When the ambulance arrived at the hospital, the doctors pronounced his father DOA. The son's guess regarding his father's health status proved correct.

But by then, the trades had been executed.

Tax-Gain Harvesting

In this ever-changing world in which we live in, there is another tax strategy known as tax-*gain* harvesting, which is precisely the opposite of the tax-*loss* harvesting strategy we just considered. What gives? How can both be tax strategies?

Tax-gain harvesting is primarily for people in lower-income tax brackets (15% or less). They can sell securities and pay the desirable 0% long-term capital gains tax rate. The idea behind tax-gain harvesting is to keep your cost basis as high as possible. That way, taxable gains will be minimized if you find yourself marooned in a higher bracket in the future. You don't get any benefit from tax-gain harvesting today; it helps shelter you from tax increases tomorrow.

Fortunately, there is no wash sale rule for capital gains. Unlike with tax-loss harvesting, you can sell a security and buy it back immediately to attach the higher cost basis.

Pay attention to which specific share lots you are selling. You may have to override your account's default cost-basis settings to make this work. You don't necessarily want to sell your lowest-basis shares; you want to sell whichever shares will let you raise the most money while generating the least amount of capital gains.

Keep in mind that you only want to harvest long-term gains. Harvesting gains at short-term rates is seldom advantageous.

You cannot realize endless capital gains with impunity. Once they push your adjusted gross income over the top of the 15% bracket, further gains become taxable. These gains can cause your Social Security benefits to be taxed. There are also your state taxes to consider. Don't go off half-cocked realizing every gain in sight just because you feel like it.

Also, this won't work if you have tax-loss carryforwards on the books. Your tax gains will just mop them up.

One more point: if you realize a gain this year selling and rebuying a security, and then next year you sell it again, you would realize a short-term gain that taxed at your marginal rate. Make sure you won't need to sell whatever you harvested for at least a year and a day.

Tax-gain harvesting will appeal to another group of people: retirees tapping their taxable accounts for living expenses. Early retirees can realize gains while in lower capital gains brackets today to immunize themselves against realizing gains in a higher bracket tomorrow after Social Security and the required minimum distributions from their IRAs begin.

From a planning perspective, if tax-gain harvesting works for you, consider whether the same headroom in your 15% capital gains bracket would be better spent doing a Roth conversion. We will talk more about these tax-planning angles later.

Dividends

Your dividends have already been taxed as earnings at the corporate level and are now taxed again as they are passed along to you, for your complete double-taxing pleasure.

There are two types of dividends, qualified and nonqualified. Qualified dividend tax treatment parallels that of long-term capital gains, per Table 3.4.

State taxes piggyback on top of these.

Nonqualified dividends are taxed at your higher marginal rate. We want our dividends to be qualified, but how exactly do they qualify?

Technically, dividends become qualified when you hold the underlying security, unhedged, for at least 61 days out of the 121-day period that began 60 days before the ex-dividend date. Translation: If you have held the security sixty-one days, you will be on velvet.

		TABLE 3.4	
Dividend tax rates by adjusted gross income, 2020			
Individual	Married	Long-term rate	+ Obamacare
< $40,000	< $80,000	0%	0%
to $200,000	to $250,000	15%	0%
to $441,450	to $496,600	15%	3.80%
> $441,450	> $496,600	20%	3.80%

When the securities are held inside a mutual fund wrapper, the mutual fund may have bought and sold them at various times even if you held the fund all year. This means mutual funds can issue a dog's breakfast (here a bad thing) of both qualified and unqualified dividends.

Some investors have margin accounts where they borrow against their holdings. Stocks held as collateral for margin— even when margin is not actually used—accrue dividends that do not receive qualified dividend status. Their dividends are taxable at short-term rates because they are loafing around on the wrong street corner and self-identifying as potentially marginable securities.

If you do not want the dividend income, a simple solution is to avoid buying dividend stocks or funds in taxable accounts. This is our standard recommendation. For these accounts, tax-alpha dogs prefer companies that buy back their own shares to those that issue dividends.

If you do buy a dividend stock or mutual fund in your taxable account, don't buy them immediately before a scheduled dividend payout, because this triggers taxes gratuitously.

All the caveats about capital gains stacking on top of ordinary income apply to dividends as well. Qualified dividends and long-term capital gains both get added to your adjusted gross income and can kick you into one of higher brackets in Table 3.4.

Investments that are Statutory Tax Shelters

Oil and Gas

Big tax breaks are available to those who own working interests in oil and gas exploration. These include the depreciation of drilling costs, the fact that working interests are considered active (not passive) income, a depletion allowance, deductibility of lease costs, exploration costs, and exemption from the Alternative Minimum Tax. The depletion allowance by itself allows the owner to write off more than the entire cost of the asset. It not only applies to oil and gas, but also timber and minerals.

The initial expenses of your working interest can be written off against ordinary income. Usually, when you get a Schedule K-1 from an enterprise in which you are not actively involved, the income and losses are passive. You can't deduct losses (e.g., real estate depreciation) from ordinary income. But with oil and gas exploration, your initial investment might be 80% deductible against ordinary income, starting year one. That deal is hard to find anywhere else.

But if you are an orthodontist in Miami, you have a problem of due diligence: how do you find a good oil and gas partnership in which to invest? The ones you don't want will be easy to find. The field is famous for scams and dubious opportunities. As is often the case when it comes to peddling tax shelters, an adage from the investment business applies: they are such terrible investments that they can only be sold to doctors.

You have to wonder why they are talking to you. If the investment were such a slam dunk, why have so many people closer to the oil patch and presumably far more knowledgeable already eschewed the opportunity?

My impression: investors get the tax deduction, but the surprise comes when the well doesn't deliver as promised. Then they are trapped in a Roach Motel: an illiquid investment worth pennies on the dollar.

Another thing to wonder about is your liability. What if Tulsa thinks your oil well has polluted their water, and the EPA wants you to spend $100,000,000 to clean it up? As the owner of a working interest, you have *unlimited personal liability in perpetuity.* Would fighting this be a great way to spend the rest of your life? That is the trade-off for the up-front tax deduction. Even if the seller blandly assures you there's some way around this—an insurance policy, an indemnification agreement, whatever—does it cover you to an unlimited extent? If insurance companies find this level of risk unacceptable, what makes you think you can afford it?

You could buy stock in Exxon Mobil (ticker: XOM). But do you want more than the market weighting that's already present in your stock market index fund? Do you have insights into the price of oil that have eluded the thousands of other people analyzing it? Presumably, Exxon Mobil's tax benefits are already included in its price.

Another option—but one that won't give you the up-front tax deduction you crave—would be to buy a publicly traded master limited partnership (MLP) that works in this space.

Master Limited Partnerships

MLPs are publicly traded limited partnerships. They typically earn 90% or more of their income from natural resource activities. Most MLPs are involved in the distribution of oil or natural gas through pipelines.

Here is the business model: they operate a toll road. The pipes have a meter, and they charge for the volume of oil or gas they pass. While they work in the energy sector, their fortunes supposedly do not depend on energy prices, because people need oil and gas delivered whether it is expensive or cheap. This makes them utilities. They have a general partner, who operates the business (with various incentives), and limited partners—you and me, the unitholders—who provide capital and receive cash distributions from the ongoing operations.

We all need energy, and these are capital-intensive industries, yet at the end of this rainbow is a low-return asset: a rate-regulated pipeline. The solution has been to lower their cost of capital by giving them a pass-through tax structure. Additionally, the depreciation of the pipeline further shelters owners from taxes. MLPs avoid the double taxation to which corporations are subject.

The distribution is not a dividend. It is a sandwich of earnings plus depreciation, less the amount of money spent on maintenance. Under the tax code, that spells return of capital. Thus, distributions—which can be 3% to 7% or more—are not fully taxed when received. They are taxed only once, primarily when you sell the units. The capital gains recognized upon sale can be huge.

The killer maneuver is to use MLPs for low-tax income in mid-to-late retirement and then let them pass through your estate for the free reset to fair market value, neatly sidestepping the recaptured depreciation and eliminating the capital gains. If you try to weasel out of the final reckoning by donating your shares to charity, for example, you only would get a tax credit for your low cost basis, not the fair market value.

When you own units in an MLP, you get stuck with a fiendishly complicated K-1 form. The MLP websites make this as painless as possible, but it's still an ordeal. TurboTax can handle it if you do it yourself, but your accountant is going to charge you for the service, and this could amount to hundreds of extra dollars, year after year.

It gets worse: these partnerships operate in a number of different states. After all the deductions are applied, the amount you owe may be too small to be liable for state taxes in all of them, but if your holdings are large, you might have to file some individual state returns as well.

Do not hold individual MLPs in a tax-deferred account or you risk having to pay unrelated business income tax—yes, even in an IRA. To own this sector in an IRA, buy companies that issue

1099s instead of K-1s. These would include stock in the general partners, such as ONEOK Inc. (ticker: OKE), Kinder Morgan Inc. (ticker: KMI), and Williams Companies Inc. (ticker: WMB).

MLPs are subject to risks: legislative risk, environmental risk, and (along with nearly all income investments) losing value in a rising interest rate environment. They were mauled by the fracking revolution. While their tax-advantaged characteristics mostly have been preserved under TCJA, we don't know what changes might be made after 2025 when the tax bill sunsets.

Real Estate

Like oil and gas, real estate is another boondoggle in the tax code. In the unlikely event that you still itemize Schedule A deductions, you can deduct the interest on $750,000 of post-2017 home acquisition debt, with older mortgages grandfathered in under the old $1,000,000 limit. Interest on cash pulled out doesn't qualify. Property tax deductions are capped at $5,000 single/$10,000 married. This is a much less good deal than before for tax alpha dogs with big mortgages and big property taxes.

You still get a $250,000 single/$500,000 married capital gains exemption when you sell your primary residence (where you have lived for two of the last five years). In a fast-appreciating area, this raises the prospect of selling a house every two years as it approaches these capital gain thresholds, balanced against the high transaction costs. You could end up moving every two years just to qualify for the exemption. Otherwise, the tax code could box you in for the duration, so that your heirs can take the step-up in basis when you die. A house can become too expensive to sell.

Investment real estate gets a better shake, and the new rules offer a lip-smacking 20% Section 199A pass-through deduction. If you have a real estate trade or business, this is definitely worth a chinwag with your accountant to investigate how you might qualify.

After the property appreciates, you can refinance to pull money out (via borrowing) tax-free. When you want to sell, you can do a 1031 exchange to swap your basis into another "like-kind" property and pay no taxes in the bargain—your low-cost basis just carries over.

A vital question is whether you are a real estate "dealer" or a real estate "investor." If you are selling property in the normal course of your business, then you are a dealer and your profits are taxed as ordinary income. On the other hand, if you a real estate investor, your profit will be taxed at lower rates as a capital gain. Deciding which you are takes the right attorney and the right CPA to determine, set up correctly from the start. You want to use professionals who deal with these issues all day long, not Harvey who does your taxes who says he can look into it for you. You might see it one way, the IRS another, so you want the big guns on your side.

While real estate sounds like a safer place to invest than the stock market, and one that offers you greater control over your destiny, this is a mirage. Real estate investors seldom account accurately for either their returns or the risks they took to earn them. They need to calculate time-weighted returns on the one side (minus a scrupulous accounting for the value of their time in addition to their other expenses), as well as the risks of using leverage, which is a sword that cuts both ways. If real estate investing were a vastly superior proposition to stock market investing, or vice versa, everyone would have figured this out a long time ago.

There are plenty of people pitching real estate syndicates of fractional ownership and private placements who would like to invite you into theirs. Because all they want is a check, this is much easier. However, money flows to the scarce good. The scarce good here is not capital; it's good investment opportunities. The people who are great at finding and developing deals can raise all the money they want within their own network. They don't need your money. The people who want your money may not be the people with whom you want to invest. Many people offering real estate deals are indifferent to the ultimate dispensation of the property (a liquidity event that may be of paramount importance to you) because they are only in it for the ongoing property management fees. You could be years into it before you discover you made a mistake. One developer told me that, apart from his own deals, the only other person he is comfortable investing with is his former college roommate. Real estate is a relationship business.

There are public non-traded real estate investment trusts (REITs), which are notoriously riddled with high fees and always seem to be on the brink of SEC investigation. There are also private REITs, which require extensive due diligence. As a general rule, any structured product that comes to you from Wall Street will be so larded with fees that you won't come out ahead except by accident.

That leaves the publicly-traded REITs as the last efficient option standing. These get some tax advantages and, as "pass-through" vehicles, are not taxed at the corporate level. They act more like hybrid real estate + stock + bond investments, rather than a pure real estate play. Most of the income they throw off is taxed as ordinary income at marginal rates, which means you should hold them in a tax-deferred account.

The problem with real estate, as with low-income housing and oil and gas and mining and timber and farming and art and private equity and hedge funds, is that even though there may be tantalizing tax breaks dangling out there, you do not have an edge unless you are in the business. Dabblers often walk away with expensive life lessons rather than money.

We will have a few words to say about real estate "Opportunity Zones" in the next chapter.

Municipal Bonds

Men of inherited wealth, some of them given to the denunciation of government in all its forms and manifestations, have shown themselves to be passionately interested in the financing of state and municipal governments, and have contributed huge sums to this end.
—John Brooks

Municipal bonds are issued by state and local governments to fund their far-flung projects. Because one branch of government supposedly cannot tax another (except when it chooses to), they pay interest that is both federally tax-exempt and tax-exempt in the state of issue. Their yields are usually lower than taxable bonds in consideration of their tax-free status, and this difference represents the implicit tax they pay every year. For this reason, you might be better off holding taxable bonds in tax-deferred accounts than holding municipal bonds in taxable accounts.

One sneaky feature of the tax code is that municipal bond income can increase the taxes you pay on Social Security income and raise your Medicare premiums, even while muni income itself remains untaxed. The only way you will know is to figure it out using tax software.

Although states do not tax their own bonds, they enthusiastically tax those from other states. Think twice before buying all your municipal bonds from your home state. You can check your state fiscal rankings online from the Mercatus Center:

https://www.mercatus.org/statefiscalrankings

It would be good politics for Congress to stick it to the 1% by removing the tax exemption from municipal income. The reason they don't is that it would destroy the market for municipal securities. This creates a problem for the congressman back home when his nephew wants the contract to build a bridge to nowhere. But anything is possible if times are desperate. No one knows what deal will be struck when the bills for our unfunded entitlement transfer programs come to roost, shortly after the TCJA expires.

You won't get rich living off municipal bond income, but it will shelter a portion of your income from taxes. Are they a good deal for you, versus buying taxable bonds of the same credit quality and duration? Take the yield the muni bond offers, and then divide it by (1 minus your marginal tax rate). This tells you the yield you would require from a taxable bond to match the yield the muni bond pays, after-tax. Check it using one of the municipal versus taxable bond interest calculators on the Internet. In a middle bracket or above, municipal bond funds are usually more advantageous.

People exposed to the Alternative Minimum Tax (and fortunately there aren't many under the TCJA) need to buy AMT tax-free municipal bonds. If you are in the highest bracket and are likely to remain there, you can eke out an extra 0.25% or so of yield by buying "private activity" bonds (e.g., to finance that vital new sports stadium in your hometown). These have higher credit risk, so the extra yield is not free. The frictional costs of trading in the bond market still make Vanguard's low-cost tax-free bond funds the go-to choice for most investors.

Insurance Products

One of the great benefits of being in an ultra-high-net-worth family is the ability to self-insure against many calamities. The rest of us need to use an insurance company to pool our risks on big-ticket items.

Whole life insurance offers you tax-deferred growth of the investment portion of your portfolio, plus a tax-free death benefit, plus tax-free distribution of your basis and tax-free (but not interest-free) loans whenever you want them.

Investors facing the estate tax (state or federal) use guaranteed no-lapse universal life insurance to move money out of their estate by buying the policy inside an irrevocable life insurance trust (ILIT). These policies can pay estate taxes or facilitate the buyout of a closely held family company.

The reason you want to buy a guaranteed no-lapse universal life policy in these cases is that you are only buying it for the death benefit. You would not be using the policy as an "investment" at all, taking loans from it or building up cash value. These policies are therefore cheaper than whole life, which makes them less desirable to sell. While they are sold as if they magically manufacture the death benefit out of thin air, there is no magic here: the death benefit comes from the premiums paid by policyholders, plus the modest investment returns. Those who die the earliest win.

Annuities: If you buy an immediate annuity with pre-tax funds, as from an IRA, all payments will be taxed as ordinary income. The annuity is considered an investment inside the IRA wrapper. The insurance company will give you an annual valuation for RMD purposes, and you will be responsible for taking the correct distribution each year. Unless—you annuitize the annuity, converting it into a string of payments based on your life expectancy. In that case, the annuity amount counts as the RMD amount. This RMD cannot be used to offset any other RMD amounts that you owe from other retirement accounts—it stands on its own.

If you buy an annuity with after-tax money, the payments will be partly taxed as ordinary income (the projected growth over your estimated lifetime) and partly an untaxed return of principal. If you live longer than your actuarial lifetime, you will be receiving all "growth" dollars taxed as ordinary income.

With variable annuities, when you pull the money out in lump sum withdrawals, the IRS makes you take out your gains first (Last In, First Out), which it is pleased to tax as ordinary income at your marginal rate. Only after these gains have been burned through do you take out untaxed return of principal.

In the unlikely event that you elect to "annuitize" your variable annuity and receive it in fixed installments, then each payment is taxed at a constant ratio of earned income/return of principal, just as with an immediate annuity.

Qualified Small Business Stock

Because the government recognizes that most people work for small employers, they have created a carve-out for investors (entrepreneurs) in such businesses.

The company:

- Must be a domestic C-corporation
- Stock is acquired directly from the company at issuance
- Under $50 million
- Not in professional services, banking, farming, mining, or hospitality

Hold the stock for five years, and the gains can be excluded from taxation. As with all such government programs, it is about assiduously following detailed rules. Most people who want the tax break won't qualify for it, but if you might, it could tip the balance towards organizing as a C-corporation rather than some other business entity. Check with your attorney. In the end, you need to weigh whether the cost of the tax planning and ongoing compliance would be less than paying capital gains taxes or getting a reset in basis at death.

The Boneyard

- To get rich, use the God-given statutory tax shelters laid out here before you like a land of dreams.
- If you can find employment within a statutory tax shelter, so much the better.
- In taxable accounts, keep your dividends qualified and your capital gains long-term.
- Harvest capital losses whenever they appear.

Chapter Four

Tax Shelters (Mostly)
for the High-Net-Worth

Since high-income types pay most of the taxes under our progressive tax code, they have the most to lose by failing to take advantage of various legal means to lower their tax bills.

Charitable Giving

The tax deduction for charitable contributions is one of the oldest sacred cows. Our income tax began 1913 and the charitable deduction followed four years later in 1917. It is a tax break for the well-heeled and is responsible for a lot of dubious charity work by nonprofits. People would rather give money to tax-deductible charity organizations where at least they get a swell dinner and their names listed as big-shot philanthropists instead of the IRS, where the giving experience often fails to spark joy.

Under TCJA, charitable donations are less valuable. With a standard deduction of $12,400 single/$24,800 married plus another $1,350 for seniors, you are unlikely to itemize deductions. An itemizing married couple who gives $25,000 to charity will only be $200 to the good vs. simply taking the standard deduction. If you are going to donate, it is better to funnel a large contribution into one year (say, $100,000 in one year rather than $25,000 a year over four years) so that more of it counts as a tax deduction.

Charitable giving is not a blank check. You can only deduct up to half your adjusted gross income (AGI) in any one year for cash donations, although you can carry forward the excess over five years after that. Donations in the form of capital gain property are typically limited to 30% of AGI. The amount is 20% if you are giving to a private nonprofit operating foundation like your family foundation. Check the IRS regulations before making a substantial gift.

Don't give cash to charities except in very small amounts (say, under $50).

If you have not started taking required distributions from your IRA, the best course is to donate appreciated securities from your brokerage account, since the charity will not have to pay any capital gains tax. This is a useful method for stripping off your low-basis shares. Just make sure that the gains are all long-term (you have held the stock over twelve months), per IRS rules. You also need a charity that is set up to accept stock. I am a fan of the donor-advised charitable funds available from Vanguard, Fidelity, and Schwab, which make this process easy.

A note about timing. If you are mailing a check to charity, the date of the contribution for tax purposes is the day you mailed it. But if you are transferring stock, the effective date is the date they receive it (or the date the transfer occurred, if you are sending a stock certificate). Don't put this off until the end of December or your plans could backfire.

When itemizing charitable donations on Schedule A, a gift of less than $250 to a charity requires either a receipt or a canceled check. A gift to a charity worth more than $250 needs a contemporaneous written acknowledgment. A non-cash gift worth more than $5,000 requires a qualified appraisal. What is that? An appraisal by a "Qualified Appraiser," who has the requisite background. The appraisal must note that it was prepared for tax purposes. If the value is more than $50,000, your appraisal will be reviewed by the IRS's own experts, who can be counted on to recognize value your appraiser may have overlooked.

Those taking RMDs can do Qualified Charitable Distributions (QCDs) from their IRAs (up to $100,000 a year). These count toward the required minimum distributions but otherwise will not be counted toward your Medicare surtax or affect the tax on your Social Security income. These QCDs must be checks sent directly from your IRA custodian to a 501(c)(3) the registered charity. You cannot give them to a donor-advised fund or a private foundation. You receive no Schedule A tax deduction by following this method; you only avoid having to pay the taxes on the IRA distribution that you otherwise would have received. A rule of thumb is to take QCDs in January and the remaining RMD the following December. If you plan to do Roth conversions, do them after your entire RMD has been withdrawn.

Private family foundations are another option for high-net-worth-types. Because they are regulated at the state level, they rarely receive scrutiny unless their abuses make headlines or someone files a complaint. Consider how frequently our politicians find their family charitable foundations in the news for flagrant abuses, and no one dares close them down. A family foundation is a great vehicle to create employment for slacker relatives, and more than one trust fund baby has found purpose in life for the first time when placed in charge of one. Private foundations can fund broadening travel experiences for family member trustees, as they go to Costa Rica to eco-zip line through the rain forest and then jet to Gstaad to study the effect of global warming straight from the slopes. For better or worse, private foundations have far more flexibility than donor-advised funds. There's no reason a family can't have both. For example, the family foundation can contribute to the family donor-advised fund (but not the other way around), and then use that fund for anonymous giving.

Low-Basis Holdings

The paradox of wealth is that people get rich through concentrated holdings, but they stay rich through diversification. Of course, there are also lots of people with concentrated holdings who never become rich, but who do manage to become poor when their concentrated holdings get wiped out. On the success side of the ledger, the concentrated holding is usually a family business worth $15 million or a big block of shares in some publicly-traded company.

When it comes to this kind of hairy low-basis assets, you have two bad choices: you sell and pay titanic capital gains taxes, or you hang by your fingernails and risk watching their value plummet by far more than the taxes you would have paid if you had you only been smart enough to sell. The academic view is that it is better to sell and diversify unless you are very old, in which case you should die at your earliest convenience so your heirs can register the step-up in cost basis.

Table 4.1 lays out the possibilities.

TABLE 4.1 Coping with a concentrated holding		
Your Action	The Business	Result
Hold	Prospers	What, me worry?
Hold	Declines	Kick yourself
Sell	Prospers	Kick yourself
Sell	Declines	Laugh at fate

Don't let this table fool you. These prospects are not equally weighted. In practice, you almost always end up kicking yourself.

What else can you do?

Charitable Trusts. Donate the asset to a charitable remainder trust (CRT) and take a tax deduction for the remainder interest. The trust sells the asset and pays no taxes. It invests the proceeds in a diversified portfolio, the purpose of which is to pay you an annuity, taxable in various IRS-mandated tiers, according to the kind of income it represents—but at a minimum avoiding the 5% jump in capital gains (between 15% and 20%) and skipping the 3.8% ACA Obamacare surtax as well.

After twenty years of this payout, or upon your death, the remainder goes to your destination charity (possibly your donor-advised charitable trust). At least 10% of the original donation must be earmarked for this purpose. If you are long-lived, or if your underlying investments perform well, you might even come out ahead versus selling the asset outright and taking the tax hit. Make your children the income beneficiaries, and this breakeven can come even sooner if they pay taxes at a lower rate than you.

With world enough and time, you can come out ahead doing well by doing good, but let's be brutally honest. In most cases, this is more of a charitable giving opportunity than the optimal wealth-building technique. A simpler approach, though even less remunerative to you, is to donate some of the shares of the low-basis asset to charity. Donor-advised funds are comfortable dealing with complex private assets, such as shares in your family business, provided the dollars make it worth their while. If this is your intention, bring them into the loop early.

Two-Year Installment Sale. Sell the family biz for a ten-year note to a trust you create with the kiddies as trust beneficiaries, then wait two years and sell the business to an unrelated party.

You pay taxes on the interest from the ten-year note (stretched out over ten years), but the capital gains taxes on the sale of the family biz are now calculated from its stepped-up basis (when you sold it to the trust two years prior), not from your original low basis. There may be additional taxes on more than $5 million annually per person, but that is the basic idea.

Use an "Exchange" Fund. Here you tap Wall Street "helpers" to take the publicly traded stock off your hands and pool it into a faux mutual fund with many other holdings from people in similar distress. You get instant tax-free diversification, but at the price of high ongoing management fees, because now you will be a captive audience for seven years.

Calculate the breakeven versus selling, paying the taxes, and buying a vanilla stock index fund. You want to know upfront how you will get out of the fund, what assets they will give you at that time, and how this will be decided at the time. The details are everything.

Exchange funds are criticized as a collection of duds—stocks that people who were in a position to know, knew they didn't want. You don't see Jeff Bezos worried about his non-diversified holdings of Amazon shares or Warren Buffett trying to offload his stake in Berkshire Hathaway.

NINGs. The Nevada Incomplete Non-Grantor trust (with versions available in a few other states as well) is a relatively new vehicle. These are for people who live in high-tax states (but not New York). You donate your asset to the trust, then sell it and diversify. You pay federal taxes as before, but the NING structure prevents your home state from reaching in to collect state taxes on the sale. This protection covers taxes on subsequent gains so long as they remain in the trust, undistributed (which would cause your state taxes to bite). Because setting up and maintaining the trust takes time and money, I wouldn't bother unless I had an asset worth $10 million.

Do you live in California? The Franchise Tax Board has not yet given this strategy a formal blessing. I would not care to be the taxpayer they single out to contest this.

"Completion" Portfolios. You keep the low-basis stock but structure the rest of your holdings using assets that have a low correlation to it. For example, when my family owned a business whose prospects were tied to the price of oil, we sold all the energy stocks in our portfolio. We could have gone further and overweighted sectors that were uncorrelated with energy. We could have gone further still and shorted oil. This requires consultation with finance professionals to get right. Although it can shield you from day-to-day market volatility, it will not protect you if you own the next Enron.

Collars. You hire Wall Street helpers to put a "protective put" against your publicly traded stock. There are many ways to skin these cats, all of them expensive. Anyone proposing this should be questioned closely about the costs. You can also sell calls to offset the price of the puts or even to try to make money on the spread. If the puts and calls aren't more than 15% away from the strike price of the stock, the whole apparatus could be viewed as a "constructive sale" by the Feds.

When you collar your shares, the clock stops. If you try it after an initial public offering, the shares will never go long term, as long as they remain collared. Dividends, if any, will be taxed as ordinary income. Claiming losses on your covered calls will be suspended until you sell the underlying security. You have entered the upside-down world, and everything works against you, tax-wise.

Can you use this "collared" asset as collateral for a loan? The IRS frowns on this, but a lot of people have tried it, and only some of them have gotten into hot water. Have a powwow with your tax advisors before trying. You don't want to become the centerfold in *IRS AGENT* magazine, or they might collar you.

In sum. Any time you put your financial advisor, accountant, attorney, and insurance broker with a private banker in a room to come up with an atomic-age tax strategy, be careful. Any of them can be dangerous on their own, but all of them together? At the very least, hire someone who speaks plain English to try to talk you out of it. You might be better off just selling your holding, taking off the rubber band to pay the damn taxes, and diversifying from there, rather than trying to put everything into some Rubik's cube to confound the taxman.

None of these methods is ideal, and all have plusses and minuses, depending on your circumstances and preferences. There may be something to be said for combining several of these bad ideas into one pu pu platter, so you are not making an all-in bet on any of them. You might live with too great a concentration in one asset, sell some shares, donate some shares to charity to offset the capital gains taxes, and structure the rest of your portfolio in ways that are uncorrelated to the primary asset, for example.

Opportunity Zones

The government believes it knows better than private markets how to direct investments to make the world a better place. In December 2017, Congress created something called "Opportunity Zones" (OZ) to develop poor neighborhoods. Here are the carrots:

- when you invest capital gains into OZ, you can postpone paying the taxes on them until 2025—(hence capital gains are the only money that you should invest)
- if you keep your money in the OZ for five years, you get a 10% discount on these capital gains taxes
- if you keep the money in for seven years you get a 15% discount
- if you keep your money in the OZ for ten years, you eliminate all future capital gains on your OZ investment

Note that you don't have to roll over the entire investment into an OZ, as with a 1031 exchange. You can cash out the principal and just invest the capital gains from the sale.

Wall Street loves the idea of being able to tie up your money for a decade at high fees (including covert fees for expenses like real estate management) with the ultimate profitability of your investment being somebody else's problem—possibly yours—a decade or more from now.

While the chance to postpone paying capital gains taxes is enticing (if capital gains must be realized), the high-risk nature of the ultimate payout dumps a bucket of ice water on the dream. That fancy hotel they plan to build in the middle of the city slum with your money? Maybe it will be jumping with full occupancy in 2030 just like their Powerpoint slide deck shows. Or, maybe it won't. You will own it either way.

OZs would be a wonderful location for new businesses with high growth potential. If you love the underlying investment, the OZ location is gravy.

Here is a map where you can find them:

https://www.novoco.com/resource-centers/opportunity-zone-resource-center/guidance/novogradac-opportunity-zones-mapping-tool

Some of these are in gentrifying neighborhoods, such as ones in Los Angeles, Portland, and Scottsdale. That could give your OZ business or real estate development a nice tailwind.

Despite the good intentions, the details ultimately will be decided by the IRS and the tax court as the numerous issues are contested. Be careful.

Portfolio Loans

How is it that rich people pay no taxes, while you slave over a hot stove all day and still end up giving a fat slice of your paycheck to Uncle Sam?

Here's how:

Imagine that your only asset in this world is a twenty-million-dollar portfolio full of low-basis stocks. Sure, you could sell the stocks to live off the proceeds, but then you would have to pay capital gains taxes of up to 36.8% (depending on your state of residence).

Try this instead: Take out a portfolio loan, using your stock portfolio as collateral. That way, you don't sell any stocks, you borrow against them instead. There is no tax owed on borrowed money, only the interest expense for the loan.

Because you have borrowed money, your portfolio is leveraged. Since the long-term trend of the stock market is up (admittedly with some ups and downs along the way), instead of watching your portfolio diminish over time as you chisel off piece after piece to sell, you watch it grow instead. Your loan balance grows as well, but your larger portfolio allows for larger payouts. Under normal circumstances (which may never happen), not only can you pull out more money, but you end up with a significantly larger estate than your account-liquidating, capital-gains-tax-paying doppelganger. When you die, your children inherit the portfolio, the loan gets repaid (selling the stock at its stepped-up basis, so still no taxes), and they are free to re-start the process.

Private banking departments are happy to set up what is essentially a riskless loan at their end, knowing that this loan will bind the ultra-high-net-worth client to them forever. Most brokerages charge ridiculously high rates on their margin loans, making this idea a non-starter.

Perhaps you are wondering—can I deduct the interest on this loan as an investment expense, like I can when I buy stocks on margin? If it were up to me, I would let you, but the answer from the IRS is no, you cannot.

Here is another non-starter: you can't put up your IRA as collateral for a portfolio loan.

While portfolio loans are usually exploited by the rich, there is no reason they cannot be taken downmarket with even a six-figure portfolio. You will pay a higher rate of interest when borrowing at lower amounts, but everything can still pencil out to your advantage.

Investors have an irrational fear of leverage, a fear I share. We seldom hear of an investor losing all their money where leverage was not involved. For a retiree, with no labor income to offset portfolio losses, leverage can be Russian roulette.

While your loan will assuredly grow and compound over time, your portfolio should keep up with it under ordinary circumstances. However, bad returns are unpredictable and could push your loan-to-value into the danger zone for enforced redemptions. Portfolio loan capital ratios are more forgiving than ordinary margin requirements, but these requirements could become more stringent as regulators respond to headline risks and political factors. The capital ratio is determined by a complex formula that becomes less forgiving as volatility rises. Nothing would be less surprising than for an all-stock portfolio to lose half of its value at some point during a 35-year loan. The stock market lost three-quarters of its value during the Great Depression, for example.

Historically, interest rates have been all over the block. In 1980, you might have had to pay over 20% in interest to borrow against your beaten-down portfolio. Borrowing costs for portfolio loans are low for the present, making this a terrific deal, but if they should rise higher than your investment returns, you end up levering a doomsday machine. On the other hand, if your long-term investment returns are higher than your long-term borrowing costs, you are golden. Low borrowing costs and maintaining a low loan-to-value ratio are the keys to making this strategy work.

This income strategy should not be used for cheap thrills. It requires regular monitoring of your investment performance, your loan-to-value ratio, and your loan rate. You have to stay on top of it in case it's time to fold your tent, pay back the loan, and go back to living off plain vanilla capital gains.

AQR Tax-Aware Alternative LPs

Hedge funds do a lot of trading, often using short positions and options, leading to a tax nightmare for their owners as all the gains pass through on Form K-1, frequently at marginal bracket rates. Count me as extremely cautious about most such offerings.

AQR Capital, a quant shop, offers a notable exception. They discovered that their computer-driven approach could be married to a computer-driven tax-optimizer. By favoring short-term losses where possible and only taking long-term gains, the tax picture for some of their hedge funds suddenly became much more benign. The partnership's funds can pass along their investment losses directly to their limited partners, for use on their individual tax returns.

For example, AQR's tax-aware market-neutral limited part-nership routinely generates short-term losses for shareholders every year, even while the fund's net asset value can increase. This fund could be a worthwhile vehicle for anyone with signif-icant short-term capital gains to offset. Their global alternative fund even generates losses to put against your ordinary business income. In both cases, the write-off lowers your cost basis in the fund. You take losses at short-term capital gains or marginal income rates today and then pay for these losses at long-term capital gains rates when the fund is sold, perhaps five or ten years from now.

AQR offers academically-sourced investing solutions, reasonable fees, and funds that are true hedges, with managed volatility and zero correlation to the stock and bond markets. The funds are complicated, and you shouldn't invest in them unless you understand the underlying strategies well enough to accept the ups and downs along the way.

Giving Stock to Children

If you are going to give $15,000 to your children every year ($30,000 married), this is another opportunity to offload some of your low-basis stock, provided your kid has a lower tax bracket than you do. Your cost basis and holding period carry over with the gift.

The problem is, if the kid is under eighteen (or a full-time student under age 24 who is not providing more than half of his support) and claimed as a dependent on your tax return, when he sells the stock, the capital gains will be taxed at the preposterous kiddie tax rates, where the top bracket kicks in at $12,950 of income. Even if he doesn't sell, it can be almost as expensive for him to hold it as for you. Under the kiddie tax rules, he cannot show more than $2,100 in dividends or interest, or else the unearned income (not the gift itself or the capital gains) is taxed at kiddie tax rates. Do not give your child investments that will generate interest or dividends more than this amount, if possible. This is a textbook case for zero dividend stocks, which we will discuss later.

These gifts cannot be made the same year you each donate $15,000 to a 529 plan, which uses up your gift exclusion for that year (or for five years, if you make the full-frontal five-year contribution during year one). Money given to the children via a UTMA/UGMA account belongs to them, not to you, and is theirs to spend once they reach the age of majority (typically 18). The child's assets will be reported to college when applying for need-based financial aid, where they are far more prejudicial than 529 plan assets.

Giving Stock to Parents

The TCJA has breathed new life into an old strategy. You can use your $11.58 million lifetime exclusion to gift highly appreciated stock to your aging mother or father. Then, when they die, you get the stocks back with a fair market value reset in basis. Shazam—capital gains begone! Gift the stock at least a year before their departure for the promised land, or else the IRS will regard this as a tax avoidance scheme and unwind it.

This idea parallels the one mentioned earlier, where they sell some of the stock to pay for a Roth conversion. Who knew how incredibly useful your parents could be? Just make sure Dad doesn't decide to marry his nurse on his death bed and leave everything to her.

Partnerships

How do you change the tax basis of a non-depreciable asset without death or a taxable event? Partnerships.
—PAUL S. LEE

The use of partnerships for tax planning is too complicated to figure out by yourself. There are nearly infinite permutations of possible sub-partnerships, loans, distributions, classes of partnership ownership, and inside and outside basis. With careful planning, some of these might have the by-product of affecting the partners' taxes favorably. It is all about the specifics of your situation. Talk to your tax attorney to learn if there are any useful angles to exploit.

Family LP

A family LP is a partnership with a business purpose that holds a very-high-net-worth family's financial assets—typically, the family business and other investments. Alternatively, some families form a limited liability company (LLC) instead.

In addition to simplifying the ownership and management of the family's assets, the family LP receives a discount to the value of its holdings for valuation purposes. Even if the family LP held nothing but cash, if you owned a 49% interest, you could not compel a liquidation or a distribution. Your partnership shares would suffer from a lack of marketability, liquidity, and control. The only thing you would get for sure is the tax liability on the partnership's earnings because you receive a Schedule K–1 and would owe taxes regardless of whether or not the partnership paid a cash distribution to cover them. How much would an outside buyer be willing to pay for a 49% interest? Not one hundred cents on the dollar, surely.

Mom and Dad can use this discount when donating units of the family LP to their children via their annual $15,000 gift tax exclusion. Even when given to young children via UGMA or UTMA accounts, the children only receive direct ownership of the units when they reach the age of majority, not a block of cash that can be quickly misspent.

The same discount applies to estate planning. The general partner often turns out to be a "key man" in the family business, further discounting the valuation in the event of his or her passing.

Looking over recent court cases, one sees a wide range of discounts applied to the value of the underlying assets. Cash is discounted at 7.5% in one case (Koons) and 32% in another

(Kelley). Securities, real estate, hard assets, and businesses show wide-ranging discounts. No one said the tax court or Federal District courts have to be consistent. The only certainty is that the IRS has these discounts in their crosshairs and that narrowing them (especially in the case of marketable securities) is a priority. Of course, a family business will always be susceptible to a range of valuations, giving you room to negotiate.

I was shocked to read the IRS recently contested a family LLC on the grounds that it was formed expressly to avoid wealth transfer taxes to the next generation. The tax court disagreed, finding that there were legitimate non-tax reasons to form such a company, including:

- relieving the decedent of the burden of managing the investments
- consolidating the investments with a single advisor to reduce volatility under a written investment plan
- educating the children to jointly manage an investment company
- avoiding repetitive asset transfers among multiple generations
- creating common ownership of assets for efficient management and meeting minimum investment requirements

- providing voting and dispute resolution rules and transfer restrictions and providing the children with a minimum annual cash flow

Some of these might apply to your family LP or LLC as well.

Family Loans

One way wealthy families stay that way is by making intra-family loans. Parents loan money to their children at the below-market Applicable Federal Rate (AFR):

http://apps.irs.gov/app/picklist/list/federalRates.html

For advanced tax alpha dogs, here is the complete hat trick:

1. Parents lend their children money

2. Children invest the money

3. Thereby allowing children to arbitrage the higher rate of return from their investments against the lower after-tax loan rate

4. Meanwhile, parents make separate $15,000 annual gifts to children and children's spouses

5. Which, because money is fungible, the children (indirectly) can apply to their loan payment

At today's AFR rate (1.94%), $15,000 would cover a $773,195 mortgage, or if Mom and Dad are both giving to both Son and Daughter-in-Law, $3,092,783—enough for the kiddies to buy a starter home. There's no reason why the same approach couldn't be used when lending smaller amounts.

Ideally, the loan would be collateralized in a specified way. The loan should be formalized and the terms strictly followed. Never forgive the payments up to the amount of the $15,000 annual exclusion: write the check and then have the children pay the interest on the loan as two separate and unrelated transactions. Use a service like National Family Mortgage to document it:

https://www.nationalfamilymortgage.com

How does the IRS view family loans? They view them as "gifts" unless you have the documentation to prove otherwise.

Dynasty Trust

This device was invented by the Rothschilds in France in the eighteenth century. The idea was to protect the Rothschild heirs from the temptations of wealth (and from their spouses and creditors) by carefully regulating access to the family fortune. The result was that, unlike nearly every other wealthy family from the period, the Rothschilds still have a family fortune.

A dynasty trust is a special trust created in a jurisdiction that has repealed the common law rule against perpetuities (such as South Dakota, Nevada, Alaska, and Tennessee, among others). This allows money to pass from generation to generation without being taxed at every transition.

The trust might be funded by using the current personal $11.58 million generation-skipping transfer tax exemption or by using the $15,000 per year tax-free gift exclusion to purchase a guaranteed universal life insurance policy. There would be competing uses for these exclusions, so this has to be part of an overall estate plan.

After that, the dynasty (or perpetual) trust functions as a family bank. Their best use is to support the family heirs in productive pursuits such as getting an education, buying a home, or starting a business. The process is formalized, with written rules and responsibilities. These distributions might take the form of interest-free loans secured by the purchased property, in the case of a house or a business, or outright grants (e.g., by forgiving a college loan after the successful completion of a college degree).

The founder's hope is that the family bank will extend the money further and do more good with it than if it were left outright to the next generation, where it risks being sliced and diced in the money/sex/drugs/gambling/lawsuit/divorce/bogus investment/bad company Veg-o-matic that family wealth is prey to. A structure like this also circumvents a lot of ill-conceived requests for money from extended family members. If they have a request to make, they submit a business plan to the trustees for consideration at the next annual meeting.

The trust itself needs a trustee(s) and an investment account and must file tax returns. This won't be as cheap as leaving money to heirs outright. The hope is that the money will last longer, be taxed less (since it avoids taxation at each generation), be better protected, and ultimately put to a more productive application than if it were distributed as a one-time outright gift.

Old Money

Now that I have whetted your appetite by discussing family limited partnerships and family loans and family banks and family private charitable foundations, let's pause and reflect on how old money tries to stay that way.

It is educational to notice how these folks arrange their lives to minimize contact with the taxing authorities. I recently met a dowager whose name, daughter's name, and granddaughter's name all began with the same letter of the alphabet. I remarked upon the fact, and she told me it allows them all to use the same monogram on everything. She wasn't kidding.

The family never sells its home in East Egg—it just gets passed down to the kids with a reset to fair market value. Frictional expenses (usually 10% or more in selling a home) are postponed indefinitely, as can be the attendant resets in property taxes. The same goes for the vacation home in Hobe Sound and the pied-a-terre in Manhattan.

The family furniture is not from Ikea. It consists of classic pieces that never go out of style, even if now they are well-used (or, to put it differently, have acquired character). When a child leaves the nest to establish a home of his or her own, the new house is furnished with rugs, art, and furniture stored in the attic of the family manse, to which it all will one day return in the circle of life. Because the attic is filled with American antique furniture, they have yet another untaxed appreciating asset on their hands.

Everything they buy is a classic, meant to last forever or until it wears out and can no longer be repaired. Fashion is considered a pathetic, white trash affectation of the lower classes and nouveau riche who pattern their empty lives after Hollywood celebrities. They would never buy jewelry that couldn't be passed down forever. Clothing is expected to do duty for decades. Sometimes they wear a signature outfit that functions as a kind of uniform, like a character from a Wes Anderson movie.

People like me who are always waiting for the next upgrade can benefit from this kind of century-long view in financial planning. In Los Angeles, we pay 10% sales tax. Old-money families loathe shopping. They hit the stores a lot less often than my family does.

I was completely unaware that such families consider prep schools and Ivy League colleges to be their family schools. "Oh, yes, everyone goes to Groton and then finishes at Harvard." To me, that sounded like something from an Edith Wharton novel, but it still holds today. This family has built long-term relationships with the schools it attends, greasing the path for each succeeding generation.

Look at how this allows an old-money family to sustain its capital. It builds up intellectual capital in its children—all untaxed. They go into the family business, or they use the family friends and connections (social capital: another super-valuable untaxed asset) from the family clubs (cultivated just like the family schools) or the family church (St. Whoever's, where they serve on the Vestry) to get a job. Another untaxed asset is the family reputation, honed by decades of low-profile good works through the family foundation. All relationships are long-term relationships. They don't marry the chorus girl or the pool boy—they marry within their class. The family also has a posse of trusted advisors, groomed over a lifetime—yet another untaxed asset—so each generation does not have to repeat the same predictable mistakes.

Family members famously (infamously) do not retire., extending their productivity for decades. All the money belongs to the family and everyone is a steward for the next generation. It's not like our modern exploded nuclear families, where everyone is out on a shrinking ice floe by themselves fending off sharks with a pole.

Does it work? Not very often. Wayward children, divorces, legal battles, and financial predators all take their toll. But it is directionally correct. It pays to live like old money, even if you are not there . . . yet.

I heard of one instance where many of the family's physical assets disappeared after the death of the surviving matriarch. The jewelry was switched with inexpensive pieces. The rugs were replaced with oriental carpets from Pier 1. The paintings gave way to posters. The antiques vanished. The celebrated wine cellar was provisioned with indifferent selections from Trader Joe's. There was not much personal property of value left to appraise for estate tax purposes. I suspect the children took everything. If so, any practice specifically undertaken to evade paying taxes due is against the law and is not to be condoned. I present this as an example of the lengths to which one old-money family may have gone in its excessive zeal to avoid burdensome taxation. This was clearly too far. But the general principle of wealth preservation through scrupulous tax minimization applies.

Offshoring Your Assets

Remember the good old days, when Granddad had a secret account in the Cook Islands where he hid the family's railroad bonds from the IRS? This doesn't work anymore. While this peccadillo was overlooked when it was confined to the upper crust, the Internet suddenly raised the prospect of the unwashed masses opening foreign bank accounts and transmitting their money overseas with the click of a mouse.

The Treasury Department's response was FATCA: the Foreign Account Tax Compliance Act. This bill put a gun to the head of foreign banks, forcing them to cough up all the details on U.S. citizens with accounts abroad. The reporting requirements are so onerous that most foreign banks have stopped taking U.S. citizens as customers (not much fun if you happen to live abroad). Meanwhile, on this side of the pond, the tax reporting for U.S. citizens with overseas accounts is suffocating: you have to fill out Forms 8938 and 114 (FBAR) every year for even modest-sized accounts, with crippling fines for simple mistakes.

Here's the message: our government does not want you to take your money out of the United States. This is not a good omen for a free country, but there it is. Bitcoin threatens to make currency controls irrelevant, which is one reason why it is under attack.

Meantime, schemes that promise to help you evade taxes by parking your money offshore are scams that will put you in the seventh level of hell with the IRS. The way most of us have to invest abroad is by owning U.S.-based foreign stock or bond mutual funds held under the watchful nose of the Treasury Department.

One option would be to own physical gold warehoused in a foreign storage vault (not a bank safe deposit box). My understanding is that gold bullion is not a "specified foreign financial asset" for reporting purposes. Please drop me a note from prison if I have this wrong.

You have to report on Form 105 when your family is taking more than $10,000 out of the country in currency or monetary instruments. You could also park paper stock certificates that do not pay dividends in a foreign vault. I suppose storing your Matisse or Stradivarius abroad would be another option.

You could also own real estate abroad. Why is upper Manhattan now owned by foreign criminals? As opposed to the good old days, when it was owned by U.S. criminals? (Just kidding!) Because real estate is a terrific way to launder money. Protect your money the Russian Mafia way—buy a condo abroad. If you generate income from it by renting it out, this is reported and taxed in the United States, of course.

In a world where having assets parked abroad would be lifesaving (i.e., something has gone very wrong with the United States, but the country where you stored your booty was okay), consider whether you could get to it and if you would choose to store sufficient value abroad for it to save you. Then, what of the opportunity cost if the disco apocalypse you fear does not materialize and we experience one of the 99% more likely benign scenarios instead? A lot has to go right when everything goes wrong for this to work.

Postcard from Puerto Rico: America's Tax Wonderland

As the U.S. Treasury Department continues to tighten its noose around offshore accounts, a new tax haven has sprung up right under its nose. Welcome to Puerto Rico—the island of Hurricane Irma, bond defaults, and Acts 20 and 22.

Puerto Rico is the same size as Connecticut but has more palm trees. Its finances are on the eve of destruction, and most of the population lives in poverty. To generate some revenues, its Legislative Assembly promotes tax breaks designed to lure the tired, poor, and tax-oppressed millionaires to its shores.

Act 22 offers new residents a 0% tax rate on dividends and interest income earned in Puerto Rico. Uncle Sam still wants his cut on dividends you receive from U.S. public companies, as well as profits from mainland private businesses, any pensions, and deferred compensation you earned in the States, and he will tax your Social Security benefits. The IRS will still take its cut from capital gains earned before your arrival, but going forward, Puerto Rico will tithe only 10% (becoming 5% if you wait ten years). This compares favorably to the top 37.1% all-in burden in California. When the time comes to shuffle off that mortal coil, there is usually no additional estate tax, either.

Act 20, meanwhile, entices "export" businesses (translation: hedge funds) to the island. These are taxed at a 4% flat rate, with earnings distributed tax-free. Compare that to the crippling taxes paid back home, and you will understand why hedge fund billionaire John Paulson has become one of the island's major developers.

So far, the U.S. taxing authorities have shown little interest. Why should they? It's not their jurisdiction. Moreover, Congress desperately wants Puerto Rico to succeed. One-quarter of the island's GDP is already a subsidy from Washington; if and when it collapses, it becomes our problem. Nor has there been much of an upsurge for Puerto Rican statehood recently, given its prodigious liabilities. These circumstances effectively put a "moat" around the island.

What's the catch? You must become a bona fide resident. You can't rent a post office box in San Juan and call it "home" while keeping a $5 million house and your real life back in Greenwich. That means being there at least 183 days a year, and let's review your credit card receipts and cell phone GPS to verify. If you love golf and twisting by the pool, then it's a perfect day for bananafish; otherwise, it can be a minimum-security prison that has you crossing the days off the calendar until you can fly back to civilization.

* * *

The Boneyard

The goal of Tax Planning 101 is to escape all federal taxes forever. As Prof. Edward McCaffery details in *The Oxford Introduction to the U.S. Income Tax Code,* this consists of three steps below. He goes so far as to maintain, "Any advisor who is not aware of this basic planning advice is committing malpractice."

- Buy capital assets that appreciate without producing taxable dividends (see Chapter 6).
- Borrow against these assets to finance present consumption (since a loan is not a taxable event).
- Leave the assets in your estate (so your heirs get a step-up in cost basis).

Chapter Five

The Stages of a **Dog's Tax Life**

Thanks to the incredible complexity of the U.S. fiscal system, it is impossible for anyone to understand her incentive to work, save, or contribute to retirement accounts absent highly advanced computer technology and software.

—Larry Kotlikoff and David Rapson

The tax alpha dog plays the long game. This means taking a lifetime view of your tax situation.

Granted, you cannot know your financial future for certain or the crocodile-infested brackets you'll be swimming in. Nonetheless, you need a plan. If you have a plan, you can always adjust to changing conditions. With no plan, you will be vamping. Don't be like the radiologist who walks into his CPA's office at age seventy and says, "OK, I have everything locked in my $6,000,000 IRA, now how do I not pay taxes?"

Your *marginal tax rate* is the percentage of tax you would pay on the next dollar of income you earn. It is the rate used in tax planning because we are always looking at what difference changing your tax strategy will make.

The tax code is progressive. It's not just that you pay more because you earn more—that would be true even with a flat tax. Rather, the more money you earn, the higher your tax rate becomes. For all the complaining about the 1%, the United States has one of the steepest tax rates on Spaceship Earth.

Table 5.1 lists the tax brackets for 2020, as a starting point. These get adjusted for inflation every year.

TABLE 5.1 IRS taxable income tables, 2020		
Individual	**Married (MFJ)**	**Tax rate**
$0–$9,875	$0–$19,750	10%
to $40,125	to $80,250	12%
to $85,525	to $171,050	22%
to $163,300	to $326,600	24%
to $207,350	to $414,700	32%
to $518,400	to $622,050	35%
> $518,400	> $622,050	37%

These brackets are like buckets that get filled up and taxed before you go to the next tier. If you are single and earn $40,126 the first $9,875 gets taxed at 10%, then the money you earn between $9,875 and $40,125 gets taxed at 12%, and the final $1 you earn gets taxed at 22%. In this case, your average tax rate would be 12%, but your marginal tax rate would be 22%. That's the key number for tax planning.

Even that is an oversimplification. There is a standard deduction of $12,400 for singles in 2020, which means the first $12,400 of your income is untaxed. You get to take on another $1,350 if you are 65 or over. But once you earn more than that, your next dollar is taxed 12%, and 12% would be your marginal tax rate. And once you earn more than $40,125 plus the standard deduction of $12,400, or a total of $52,525, your next dollar is taxed at 22%. And so on, as you climb up the brackets, filling each tax bracket bucket along the way.

The tax brackets for ordinary income are just a first cut. You also take into account your credits and deductions, your capital gains and dividends, taxes on Social Security benefits, the Alternative Minimum Tax, the ACA Obamacare surtax, and the impact of all these on your Medicare premiums. If this nightmare were replaced by a flat tax, as sensibly advocated by the *New York Times* back in 1992, life would be simpler and more productive. You could file your tax return on a postcard.

Henceforth, what is the purpose of your life? Tax bracket management.

Capital Gains and Dividends

We just saw how your ordinary income gets taxed as you rise through the brackets. It works the same way with long-term capital gains and qualified dividends.

TABLE 5.2 CG & Dividend tax rates by Adjusted Gross Income, 2020			
Individual	Married	Long-term rate	+ Obamacare
< $40,000	< $80,000	0%	0%
to $200,000	to $250,000	15%	0%
to $441,450	to $496,600	15%	3.80%
> $441,450	> $496,600	20%	3.80%

If you were single and all the money you had this year was $40,000 of capital gains, you would owe zero tax. Even better, because you have a standard deduction of $12,400, you could earn up to $52,200 of dividends and capital gains and pay zero tax. You would be taxed at 15% on the next dollar of capital gains or dividends after that, all the way up to $200,000 (plus your standard deduction, or $212,400). Then, because you have crossed the next bracket line, your next dollar of capital gains is taxed at 18.8%. And so on as the capital gains & dividend buckets get filled up.

Under TCJA, the highest tax rates for income no longer align with the top rates on dividends and capital gains. They kick in much sooner, while you are still in the 32% bracket for income.

Beware the Capital Gains & Dividends Bump Zones

Notice the heading in Table 5.2. Your capital gains and dividend tax rate is not tied to the amount of your dividends and capital gains, but to your adjusted gross income, which includes your ordinary income plus your capital gains and dividends. As Michael Kitces has pointed out, the effect of this parlor trick is that ordinary income is taxed twice. It is taxed once as ordinary income, and then once more as it pushes the capital gains and dividends stacked on top of it into higher brackets.

Let's walk through an example to lay bare how evil this is.

Imagine that you had ordinary income of $12,400, which is exactly the point at which you pay zero tax (because of the standard deduction). Your next dollar of ordinary income would be taxed at 12%.

Now add to this $40,000 of capital gains and dividends, exactly to the point where you would pay zero tax. Your next dollar of capital gains and dividends would be taxed at 15%.

What happens when you add another dollar of ordinary income? You would expect it to be taxed 12% because that is now your tax bracket. But since the tax code stacks capital gains and dividends on top of it, what really happens is that your next dollar is taxed 12% as ordinary income plus generates 15% in new taxes as it pushes up your capital gains, for a total marginal tax of . . . 27%! Inside what looks for all the world like a 12% ordinary income and 0% capital gains bracket, you have suddenly gone from a marginal rate of 0% on your last dollar to a marginal rate of 27% in a single bound, without adding a penny of dividends or capital gains.

Worse, the 27% bracket continues right to the top of the fake 12% bracket. You can't shake it until you get $52,525 of ordinary income, where your marginal tax rate drops from 27% to 22% because you have graduated to the 22% bracket.

"By the way, I notice that even though you are supposedly in the 12% tax bracket, you actually rack up a 27% marginal rate. Why don't you move a few things around to raise or lower your income this year so you only pay tax at the 12% rate?"—said no one's accountant ever.

There are other bump zones, large and small, whenever your specific concoction of income and deductions cause your capital gains and dividends to be taxed at a higher bracket rate.

By the time you calculate the exact answer in April it will be too late to do anything about it for the previous year unless you also have a time-traveling DeLorean.

The tax code is highly personalized and interactive, just not in a good way. Your marginal tax rate does not rise smoothly. Finding your rate is like shooting a ball into a pinball machine. You watch it getting slingshot around the board, lighting lights, buzzing buzzers, ringing bells and spinning spinners, falling into holes, hitting bumpers and flippers, and only at the end can you look up at the game board to find out how much you owe.

Fire up TurboTax or call your accountant and have him plug in your estimated numbers no later than December, while there is still time to do something about them. Don't forget to include your projected year-end capital gain and dividend distributions from your stocks and mutual funds. Estimate your tax liability as it stands, and then add another $100 of ordinary income side to see how much your taxes rise. Do they go up $27? That means you are in a 27% marginal rate. Unbelievably, once Social Security is stirred into the pot, you can face a marginal tax rate of up to 49.95%—pretty close to 50%—all while assuming you are safely nestled in the 12% tax bracket.

Riding the Brackets

Problem one: you will cross a number of tax brackets over your lifetime. But the time you spend in the higher brackets hurts because the tax code is steeply progressive. You especially will not like the regulation GI haircut you get at the top. Table 5.2 highlights some key thresholds to stay under if you can. Note that these are after your deductions, which would give you an extra $12,400 single/$24,800 married to maneuver in most cases. Your thresholds will depend on your unique cocktail of earnings and deductions.

TABLE 5.3 Some 2020 key thresholds to stay under			
Penalty	**Single**	**Married**	**Result**
Medicare B Surcharge	-	$750,000	Premium rises 240%
Bracket jump	$518,400	$622,050	40.8% short-term CGs
Top bracket	$518,400	$622,050	35% to 37% rate
Medicare B Surcharge	$500,000	-	Premium rises 240%
Cap Gains & Divs	$441,450	$496,600	20% bracket on CGs & Divs
Bracket Jump	$207,350	$414,700	32% to 35% marginal rate
Bracket Jump	$207,350	$414,700	38.8% short-term CGs

TABLE 5.3 (CON'T) Some 2020 key thresholds to stay under			
Penalty	Single	Married	Result
Bracket Jump	-	$326,600	27.8% short-term CGs
Bracket Jump	-	$326,600	24% to 32% rate
Medicare B Surcharge	-	$326,000	Premium rises 220%
Medicare B Surcharge	-	$272,000	Premium rises 160%
Medicare Tax	$200,000	$250,000	0.9% surtax earned income
Obamacare Tax	$200,000	$250,000	3.8% surtax on CGs & Divs
Bracket Jump	$163,300	-	24% to 32% rate
Medicare B Surcharge	$163,000	-	Premium rises 220%
Medicare B Surcharge	$136,000	-	Premium rises 160%
Medicare B Surcharge	$109,000	$218,000	Premium rises 100%
American Opportunity	$90,000	$180,000	College tax credit expires
Medicare B Surcharge	$87,000	$174,000	Premium rises 40%
Bracket Jump	$85,525	$171,050	22% to 24% rate
Lifetime Learning	$69,000	$138,000	Grad school credit expires
Bracket Jump	$40,126	$80,250	12% to 22% rate
Cap Gains & Divs	$40,000	$80,000	15% tax on CGs & Divs

TABLE 5.3 (CON'T) Some 2020 key thresholds to stay under			
Penalty	Single	Married	Result
Saver's Credit	$32,500	$65,000	Credit phase out ends
Saver's Credit	$19,250	$39,000	Credit phase out begins
Bracket Jump	$9,875	$19,750	10% to 12% rate

Of all these tax jumps, the most insidious is the $200,000 single/$250,000 Medicare surtax on income (0.9%) and the ACA Obamacare surtax on capital gains and dividends (3.8%). These are not indexed to inflation, because Congress knows Medicare is hopelessly underfunded, so the surtax is designed to ensnare the middle class eventually.

Otherwise, the major discontinuities to watch out for are the bracket leaps from the 12% to the 22% tax bracket and from the 24% bracket to the 32% bracket.

The Medicare Part B surcharges in Table 5.3 are based on your Modified Adjusted Gross Income from two years earlier and represent the increase over the base premium of $144.30/a month. A couple in a low bracket would pay $103,176 for Medicare Part B over a 30-year retirement while a high earning couple would pay $350,798 for the same coverage, assuming rates do not increase (which they surely will). You can appeal the surcharge to Social Security based on life events, such as marriage, divorce, death of a spouse, or work termination. That might help during the two years waiting for the reset to occur naturally.

* * *

With that as a preamble, we will look at your tax picture over your lifetime—first by life stage and then by tax bracket.

Working Life

Unless you are a wealthy playboy like Bruce Wayne, you may have to work for a living. There's no shame in this—why, I happen to be a working man myself. The typical progression is that you start earning a low salary in your twenties, then it ramps up over your thirties and forties, finally leveling out in your fifties as your skills and connections deteriorate compared with the young Turks they can now hire for half your salary.

Many other career paths are possible. You might have a career where the income is not high, but the paycheck is steady. Or, you might hopscotch through a half-dozen careers over your lifetime as one fizzles out and a new one takes off.

If possible, practice tax bracket arbitrage. Take taxable income from your high-bracket years and reroute it into your low-bracket years, so that your overall tax rates stay as smooth and as low as possible. Try to fill the lower brackets to the top where this can siphon away income that otherwise would raise you into a higher bracket later.

To defer income and accelerate deductions:
- defer year-end compensation and bonuses
- postpone dividends from your C-corporation
- delay sending out year-end bills
- hang on to incentive stock options
- harvest capital losses
- make an installment sale
- buy CDs and Treasury bills that don't pay interest until they mature next year
- max out your 401(k) and deductible IRA contributions
- make a charitable donation
- tap your home equity line of credit
- write off bad debts

To accelerate income and defer deductions:
- take strategic dividends from your C-corporation
- sell your business for cash today
- harvest capital gains

- make IRA withdrawals (penalty-free over age 59½, and even earlier with 72(t) distributions
- Roth IRA conversions
- exercise stock options
- pay off your home equity line of credit
- sell your accounts receivable to a factoring company
- throw any business-related bills into the furnace—then claim they were lost in the mail, and reassure your creditors you will pay them just as soon as you return from Earth orbit on January 1

Apart from tax-bracket arbitrage, here are some suggestions that might apply, depending on your situation:

- Because being married is generally penalized by the tax code (especially for those with high incomes), if married you would be, get married in January rather than December. In December, you will be taxed as if you had been married for the entire year, even if you were only married for two weeks.
- Late in life, follow attorney Josh Rubenstein's advice: "No matter how unprincipled you think marriage is, consider marrying your long-term partner to qualify for the deceased spouse's unused exemption."

- The greatest tax break in America is employer-sponsored health insurance. It is pure untaxed compensation, as you will quickly discover if you ever need to pay for this insurance out-of-pocket.
- Your fringe benefits are another form of untaxed compensation.
- In a steady-state, low-bracket career, practice tax-gain harvesting in taxable investment accounts to protect yourself from future tax increases.
- In the early rungs of a high-paying career, contribute to a Roth IRA while you are still in a low bracket. This is basically everyone when they first enter the labor market.
- Contribute to a Health Savings Account as a backdoor retirement account whenever you are eligible. Invest it in the stock market and leave it alone to compound until late in life.
- In general, top off your contributions to tax-qualified accounts every year (IRAs, 401(k)s, and their ilk). This pockets any free employer match and locks in an immediate tax deduction.
- Over time, if your investments overflow your qualified accounts into a taxable brokerage account, rebalance your

holdings with asset location in mind, placing the bonds in your retirement plans and the stocks in your taxable account. This will set up your retirement tax profile more efficiently.

- A working spouse can contribute to a "spousal IRA" (Roth or Traditional) for a nonworking spouse.

- A high earner who can contribute to an after-tax 401(k) should consider this option. It will roll over into a Roth IRA later.

- Young people should not give to charity except in token amounts—there are just too many other super-valuable uses for their marginal dollars. Charity is a rich man's sport. Earn a lot of money when you are young and give to charity after you are well-established. Let the charity assume some of your career risk, since they will be the beneficiaries.

- As an executive, you might be able to put a portion of your income into a nonqualified deferred compensation plan, where it will compound tax-free until you receive it decades hence. Even absent such a plan, possibly you can defer your bonus or defer exercising incentive stock options.

- If you own a mix of shares plus options, "swapping" can spice up your tax life. By delivering your existing shares (if held for two years) to pay for exercising your stock options (your new shares), you avoid having to pay capital gains taxes on the shares you already owned. Your cost basis from the old shares will carry over to the fresh new ones.

- Use the reports at Stockopter.com to pinpoint a good time to exercise your stock options, so you don't leave money on the table. Call your CPA before exercising, as these events have significant tax consequences that vary depending on what kind of options you have: nonqualified, incentive, restricted stock, or restricted stock units. Once you exercise your options, immediately sell enough of the stock to bank the resulting tax bill, even at the price of triggering short-term capital gains.

- With a side hustle (speaking, teaching, consulting) where you earn consistent but not-currently-needed income, you can shelter income from current taxation with a defined benefit plan.

- If you hold dividend stocks in your taxable accounts, make sure you are not automatically reinvesting the dividends as retirement comes over the horizon. The same goes for mutual funds: stop reinvesting their interest, dividend and capital gains distributions.

Net Unrealized Appreciation of Company Stock

If you have company stock inside your 401(k), you should make a calculation.

Option 1: Roll the whole thing over to your IRA, and then pay taxes on your distributions at marginal rates when you pull the money out.

Option 2: Roll your 401(k) over to your IRA as above, but roll your company stock over to a taxable account (an account where it will not commingle with any other company stock you own).

This rollout in option 2 is a taxable event. You pay taxes at your current marginal rate on your cost basis in the company stock. After that, when you sell the company stock, you pay taxes on the capital gains at capital gains rates.

P.S. Don't do this under age fifty-five, because you would have to pay a 10% penalty on any taxable distribution from your 401(k). When leaving mid-career, don't touch a 401(k) with company stock until you are fifty-five and can distribute it to a taxable account without paying the penalty. Most companies will not let you roll your other 401(k) assets over to your IRA and just leave the company stock inside it. It's all or nothing.

To determine your best course of action, run the decision by your accountant.

Relocate

If you haven't yet moved to Puerto Rico, consider relocating to a tax-friendly retiree hamlet. While low state income tax rates are widely touted bait for retirees, weigh the total tax burden: state and local taxes, property tax, personal property tax, sales tax, and fees for local services. Several states have an estate tax or an inheritance tax, and some have both. See Tables 7.2 and 7.3 in the last chapter for the latest naughty list. These would be great places to avoid dying if you have enough money to get their attention ($1,000,000 at the low end).

The Twilight Zone: Post-Retirement, Pre-Required Distributions

Imagine that you retire before age seventy. Your paycheck is behind you, and your income from Social Security and RMDs from your retirement accounts lies in the future. This brings you to an enchanting rest stop on the highway of life.

Possibly, you have just fallen off a tax cliff—in a good way! You could be in a 10% or 12% tax bracket and a 0% dividend and capital gains bracket for the first time in decades, with no income to speak of, especially if you have prepared to live off cash savings or withdrawals of principal from your taxable accounts. Having significant cash reserves at this time can be useful in guarding against "sequence of returns" risk (when selling stocks in a downturn during early retirement causes the account to fail prematurely) and lets you do Roth IRA conversions without having to draw from the amount converted to pay the taxes. Instead of shoveling more money into the stock market during your final working years, it might be smarter to bankroll some cash, especially if Roth conversions loom ahead.

This presents the opportunity to do some resourceful tax planning. If you are in a lower bracket now than you will be after you begin taking both Social Security and RMDs, this is a great time to pull money from your Traditional IRA accounts up to the top of today's lower bracket.

Your 401(k) Plan

While these plans have improved considerably, I generally advocate rolling them over to an IRA, where you have better investment choices. A Roth 401(k) might have mandatory RMDs, while a Roth IRA will not. However, 401(k) plans are covered by ERISA provisions and can offer better protection from creditors than an IRA (IRA creditor protections are highly variable, depending on your state of residence). If asset protection is important, staying with the 401(k) for the time being might be a better idea.

Under the Secure Act, your 401(k) is treated like a Traditional IRA both for RMDs and after you depart earth life. Your spouse can take the RMDs over her lifetime, but younger adult heirs will be forced to pull them out over ten years. It is possible that your plan documents contain other restrictions. Talk to your plan administrator to ascertain the options for beneficiaries if you decide not to roll your plan into an IRA.

If your 401(k) has any Roth or after-tax contributions, the custodian needs to make two rollovers: the pretax amount to a rollover IRA and the post-tax amount to a Roth IRA. Make sure your 401(k) administrator does this correctly. Don't let them mail you a check. This should be a custodian-to-custodian back-office transfer.

IRA RMD Tax Bracket Creeps

While you are working, you make all these psychedelic tax-deductible contributions to your retirement plans. Then you retire, and you're rockin' and boppin' until one day when you're seventy (or seventy-two under Secure Act) and Uncle Sam says (knock knock), "Here I am!" and forces you to start pulling money out on his rate schedule and timetable. Now everything gets thrown into reverse. Your IRA disgorges more and more taxable income every year, and you stand by powerless to stop it.

These are called required minimum distributions (RMDs), and they are taxed as ordinary income at your marginal rate. The process starts innocently enough, but then it ramps up over time. You might have to pull out more money than you need just for the taxing pleasure of your investment partner, the IRS.

By now you are also cashing a Social Security check. Combined with anything else you have coming in from your taxable accounts, part-time work, rents, pensions, delayed compensation, annuities, inherited beneficiary IRAs, plus any of the above from your spouse, this income conspires to push you into higher tax brackets. It will not be a problem for most people, who are retiring on empty and don't expect to be taxed much on their withdrawals. But what about you, tax alpha dog? Was this your dream for a relaxing, stress-free retirement: being heavily taxed by the IRS?

This is why we recommended that you keep stocks in taxable accounts and bonds in tax-deferred accounts. We want most of the growth to occur in taxable accounts where it won't end up getting taxed as ordinary income.

You especially want to guard against this if rising RMDs (which could double over your retirement) will hoist you into a higher bracket. This becomes very costly for those who might trespass from the 12% to the 22% bracket, or from the 24% to the 32% bracket. If this could be you, it is worth a close analysis to determine your best strategy.

If RMD bracket creep is going to create problems, the way to address it is through a series of partial Roth conversions up to the top of a lower tax bracket early in retirement. People make the mistake of thinking of Roth conversions as an all-or-nothing affair, but the cool kids convert small amounts year after year. By paying more taxes today, you can end up paying significantly less tax over your lifetime. The net effect of the TCJA has been to make Roth conversions more attractive since we are paying taxes today at lower rates than those slated to reappear when the TCJA sunsets in 2025.

Another option is to pull out money from your IRA today (at lower tax rates) and put it in your taxable account. If you are under 59½ and foresee that required IRA distributions are going to push you into higher brackets in later retirement, a 72(t) distribution lets you pull money out of your IRA penalty-free (but not tax-free) in substantially equal periodic payments derived from an IRS table based on your expected lifespan. With a 401(k), you can pull money out with no penalty after you turn 55 and have left your employer. These address the bracket creep issue equally as well as a Roth conversion. Either approach means the IRS's distribution table will be applied against a lower IRA account balance, resulting in smaller forced withdrawals later (though at the price of a higher income taxes today).

As a rule of thumb, you are generally safe to do Roth conversions or IRA withdrawals up to the top of your current tax tier. In other words, if you are in the 12% bracket now, you will likely be in the 15% bracket once the TCJA sunsets. If you are in the 22% bracket or the 24% bracket, you have a lot of headroom up to the top of the 24% bracket, and other things equal that will still be cheaper than paying taxes at 25% or 28% after TCJA sunsets. Roth conversions can even work in the 30% brackets, but the price is potentially high, as there is no top to the 37% bracket.

The goal is to smooth out the taxes over your entire retirement, keeping them as low as possible for as long as possible. Spend no time at all in higher tax brackets when this could have been prevented by proactive tax management earlier.

State taxes count, too. If you are presently paying an additional 9.9% in Oregon state taxes on your Roth conversions, but plan to retire to Nevada where you will pay no state taxes at all, this affects the calculation.

Touchingly, the IRS provides a more lenient RMD table for married couples where one partner is more than ten years younger than the other. If you are currently married to someone closer to your own age, you might benefit from marrying someone much younger. When rockabilly star Jerry Lee Lewis married his 13-year-old cousin, it caused a scandal, but think how advantageous his IRA distributions would have been had the marriage lasted. The same is true for Hugh Hefner's wife Crystal, who was sixty years younger than Hef and now must be milking the IRS Joint Life Expectancy Table for all its worth. When Hefner once asked a young playmate on a date, she told him she had never dated anyone over thirty before. He replied, "That's okay, neither have I." His broad-minded approach worked well to optimize his retirement account RMDs.

Taxable Account Capital Gains Creeps

You are not out of the woods yet. You may have a large taxable account that houses unrealized capital gains that are growing every year. As you draw down the account for living expenses, you will pull out principal and sell your high-basis shares first, but increasingly over time, you will draw from the elixir of pure capital gains. This can force you into a higher capital gains bracket when you cross the lines shown in Table 5.3.

TABLE 5.3 Capital gains bracket thresholds, 2020		
Single	Married	CG+NIIT tax rate
< $40,000	< $80,000	0%
to $200,000	to $250,000	15%
to $441,450	to $496,600	18.8%
> $441,450	> $96,600	23.8%

If you are in a lower capital gains bracket today but foresee crossing into a higher one later, the maneuver is tax-gain harvesting: prophylactically realizing more gains today (paying more taxes earlier at lower rates) to realize less gains in higher brackets later.

The question arises: are you better off exploiting the limited headroom to the top of your next tax bracket by doing a partial Roth conversion in your IRA or by doing tax-gain harvesting in your taxable account?

Other things equal, partial Roth conversions are more desirable since they lower your required minimum distributions and give you access to the funds later by letting you withdraw from your Roth tax-free. Additionally, Roth withdrawals don't affect your Social Security taxes or raise your Medicare surcharges. If your heirs' tax rates are higher than yours, that also favors the Roth conversion. Tax-gain harvesting can result in taxes that you might not need to pay at all since these assets receive a step-up in basis when you die.

Michael Kitces suggests that you start by doing a Roth conversion up to the amount of your standard or itemized deductions until you pay zero tax at your marginal rate. You want to pay as much tax as you possibly can in the zero percent bracket. Keep all sources of income in mind as you calculate this.

After that, it is hard to beat zero tax on capital gains, so harvest capital gains up to the point where they become taxable as well: $40,000 for singles and $80,000 for marrieds. Qualified dividends also count towards these limits, so leave room for these as well as any year-end dividend and capital gain distributions from your mutual funds.

Solve for Everything at Once

In the good old days, many Americans didn't have to worry about either saving for retirement or managing their retirement income because their lifetime of employment at a benevolent company took care of both via a professionally-managed company pension plan.

Now we must do both ourselves, delivering us into the arms of a smiling financial services industry eager to extract as much in fees from us as possible. In theory, the saving side ("accumulation") can be done using index funds, although most investors fail even this test. People get the index fund fever only to backslide into ad hoc market timing and performance chasing.

The retirement spending side ("decumulation") is vastly more complicated. A number of websites give guidance on the so-called safe withdrawal rate that can be wrenched from a portfolio, but the correct order in which to draw down the accounts and the questions of whether, when and how much should be converted to Roth IRAs along the way is highly problematic.

Most of what we read about the correct withdrawal order from your retirement accounts is wrong. It is not consistent with the latest academic research, yet it has achieved a spurious validity from having been repeated so often. For example, you may read that you should spend your taxable account first, then your IRA, and finally your Roth. Another popular approach is to spend your taxable account first, then your Roth, and finally your traditional IRA. These answers are both wrong.

The General Answer

Unfortunately, there is no general answer available for how you should draw down your accounts in retirement and do Roth conversions along the way. Every "rule of thumb" has exceptions depending on the facts and circumstances. With 10,000 baby boomers retiring every day, this is a gaping hole in our knowledge, and the shame lies with our universities, academic journals, and financial institutions for failing to come up with an integrated solution.

Financial planning software is not what it should be. As a society, we are happy to spend billions on computer games while a mere pittance spent developing this software would let the baby boomers retire with the best shot at not going broke. What we need is a solution that takes into account the possible variance in our longevity, future investment returns and tax rates and inflation, and finds the sweet spot (if there is one) where Roth conversions and the drawdown sequence and asset allocation and asset location seem the most economically advantageous.

The Specific Answer for Your Situation

It might be that converting all your IRAs to Roths is the best strategy, or it might be that keeping all your money invested in traditional IRAs is the best strategy, or it may be that the solution lies somewhere in between, by doing partial Roth conversions.

To find out, look at all the assets in each of your (and spouse's) investment accounts, including their cost bases, then plot their growth trajectory both gross and net of inflation over your remaining lifetimes, along with all your other sources of income. Then consider your projected spending and bequest motives. Finally, throw all of these against your predictions for the tax code for yourself, spouse and heirs.

Pay special attention to your projected marginal tax rate during key years:

- this year
- any year you might expect a special chunk of taxable income
- the last year you work
- the first year you retire
- the year you start Social Security
- the year you start any pensions or annuities
- the year you start RMDs from your IRA
- any year your RMDs trip you into a new tax bracket
- the year your RMDs max out
- All the above for your spouse, which will overlap with yours in provocative ways
- The year 2026, after the TCJA sunsets and we revert to the old, higher tax rates

Don't forget:

- The year after you die, and your spouse is filing single, or
- The year after your spouse dies, when you are filing single

- The marginal tax rate for your heirs after they have inherited your estate

What part of this sounds easy? There are thousands of possible solutions. The strategies that have you paying the lowest taxes may or may not be the ones that are the most economically advantageous overall. It is worth paying more taxes if the net result is that you (or your family) end up with more money in the long run. You won't be able to figure this out at the kitchen table with a pencil and a yellow legal pad.

When working with clients, I use a program called Income Solver. There is a retail version available to the public called Income Strategy. It has plenty of limitations, but it is currently the best solution that I have seen.

https://www.incomestrategy.com

If your finances are complicated and the numbers are large, pay for the higher tiers of service that offer phone support, especially as you put together your initial plan. It won't be cheap, but you will be able to see what happens to every dollar and can weigh the nuanced trade-offs between alternative strategies. Most importantly, you can get someone expert who works with these plans all day long to look over your shoulder and say, "Yes, but have you thought about this . . . ?"

Any computer that compares the lower rates under TCJA with the higher rates scheduled to take hold when TCJA sunsets in 2025 is going to love the idea of doing Roth conversions under the TCJA regime. This advantage will grow if taxpayers are saddled with even higher income tax rates when our country's unfunded entitlement crisis unfurls over the coming decades.

When doing a series of partial Roth conversions to prevent RMD bracket creep, the first move is to get stocks or other high-growth assets out of your Traditional IRA and into the Roth. Your goal is the leave the Traditional IRA stuffed with low growth assets (such as bonds), so your RMDs will grow with inflation but not much more, detaching the growth of your stocks from mandatory distributions taxed at ordinary income tax rates.

The decision to pay taxes early for a Roth conversion is emotionally fraught, no matter what the tax analysis says. Some people love the idea of Roth IRAs more than they hate paying taxes early; others hate paying taxes early more than they love the prospect of Roth IRAs. Attorney Natalie Choate suggests:

- If you don't need the RMDs for consumption, a Roth will preserve your tax-deferred compounding longer and be a better asset for heirs (especially high-bracket beneficiaries). In other words, the best people to do Roth conversions are those who don't need the money in the first place.

- If you do decide to convert, opt-out of tax withholding on the conversion amount. You want to convert as high a dollar amount as you can and pay the taxes from outside holdings.
- Ideally, you will spend outside assets to pay the taxes for a Roth conversion, leaving you with better net creditor protection, to the extent that your state shelters retirement accounts.
- A Roth conversion can lower your estate taxes, by removing the money paid in taxes (even in "contemplation of death") from your estate.
- It is always a mistake to leave a Roth to charity since the charity would never have had to pay taxes on the money in the first place. In effect, you have made the government your charity.
- You will have a more diversified tax profile with some assets in all three types of accounts, and a greater ability to control your income year-by-year to stay under the various trigger points.
- Roth accounts are better for people who expect to be long-lived.
- Congress may chip away at the Roth tax-free feature set.
- If you convert before Q4, remember that you may owe estimated taxes on the conversion.

And here are a few thoughts cribbed from IRA guru Ed Slott:

- A Roth works for anyone naming a discretionary trust as beneficiary—it removes the trust tax problem (although not on the subsequent earnings on undistributed income within the trust)
- If you have high deductions, tax credits, net operating losses, or unfilled low brackets—these are great years to convert. But not capital gains losses—they cannot offset Roth conversions beyond the $3,000 deduction applicable to ordinary income.
- If you need the money, don't convert.
- If you don't trust the government to keep its end of the deal, don't convert.
- The Roth conversion will increase your income during the year of conversion, including possible hidden taxes on Social Security and Medicare, but only for that year.
- Roth conversions, depending on their level, might either help or hurt the eligibility of some taxpayers to take the Section 199A Qualified Business Deduction.
- Teenagers should stop taking pictures of their food and open a Roth IRA.

After Age Seventy-Two: Playing the Back Nine

The big custodians will automatically calculate and make your RMD distributions if you so instruct them, which is recommended because there is a 50% penalty (!) if you screw it up. I have heard that the IRS can be forgiving if you miss the deadline, as long as you have a good story—illness, travel—but overall the agency is not noted for its Mother Teresa–like compassion.

Everyone in financial services except me seems to take the month of December off. The people left behind to answer the phones when everyone else has left to party on St. Bart's are not always the A-team. Getting accounts serviced in the closing hours of the year can be iffy. Automate your RMD and schedule it no later than mid-December so you get the maximum deferred compounding but still have time to jump on the phone if anything goes awry.

Exception: if you plan to do Roth conversions during a year when you are taking an RMD, the first money out of the IRA that year is presumed to be the RMD. Take the RMD first, then do the Roth conversion.

If you are still working after the age when your RMDs begin, and you have never been a 5% or more owner of your employer, you can postpone taking RMDs until after you retire. You also can postpone distributions from any IRAs that you may have rolled into your employer's 401k plan. Interestingly, there is no legal definition of "retirement." Part-time work might qualify as continued employment. If you wait until January 1 to finally retire, you will avoid having to take a distribution the previous year.

After the RMDs begin, you can no longer contribute to a Traditional IRA. If you are still working, you can contribute to an employer plan or SEP-IRA or Solo 401(k) of your own, though. You can rollover money from employer plans into your Traditional or Rollover IRAs.

If you work past full retirement age, instead of contributing to your retirement plan at the earliest opportunity, make your contribution between January 1 and April 15 of the following year. That way, the year-end size of your retirement account will be smaller, and so will your RMD.

Inherited IRAs: these play by their own rules. They cannot be converted to Roth IRAs. They cannot be rolled into your other IRAs. While you can take RMDs from any of your Traditional IRAs as long as the total amount of the RMDs for each one of them is included in your total, the RMDs from Inherited IRAs do not apply to your other Traditional IRAs and each one must be taken separately. Be sure to set up beneficiaries for any IRAs that you inherit.

Rollover IRAs: these are Traditional IRAs funded with money from qualified employer plans. They may have better protection from creditors, depending on state law. If that is true in your state and this extra protection is important to you, pull their RMDs from your other IRAs first.

Some people have proposed to avoid their RMDs by rolling over their plans from one custodian to another over Dec. 31, so that technically, the value of the plan at either custodian on that day is $0, thus making next year's RMD $0. A cute idea, but it doesn't wash with the IRS, sorry.

Paying Estimated Taxes with your RMD

Taxpayers over 72 who owe estimated taxes every quarter can pay these with their RMD instead. Let's say you owe $100,000 in estimated taxes, and (conveniently for this example) also have an RMD of $100,000. Instead of writing a check for $25,000 to the U.S. Treasury on April 15, June 15, September 15 and January 15, have you entire RMD paid on 12/31 with 100% withheld for federal taxes. The secret is that an RMD paid in Q4 counts as having been spread evenly throughout the four quarters of the year.

Qualified Charitable Distributions

Taxpayers paying RMDs can direct their IRA custodian to donate up to $100,000 of their RMD from a Traditional IRA (not an employer plan or SEP IRA) straight to a 501(c)(3) charity (not a private foundation or donor-advised fund). Here are the possible advantages:

- Avoiding bracket creep and the 3.8% Obamacare surtax for capital gains
- Avoiding Medicare Part B Premium surcharge creep
- Lowering the threshold for deducting medical care expenses
- The donation does not count towards percentage-of-income limits on charitable donations
- You can still take the full standard deduction, vs. having the standard deduction count against your Schedule A itemized charitable contribution

You are not allowed to receive anything of value back from the charity in compensation for this gift—not even a toothpick—or the entire QCD will be disallowed. A friendly smile and a hearty handshake from the development officer is probably okay. Your home state may not share your penchant for charitable giving and might tax you on the entire RMD amount.

You can mix a QCD with a regular IRA withdrawal to satisfy your overall RMD that year. What you don't want to do is withdraw money from your IRA, pay taxes on it, and then write a check to charity, since that same money could have been given directly to charity tax-free.

Surviving Spouse

The tax code forces an agonizing decision on you at the worst possible time. For the year you become a widow plus the next one, you can file a joint return. After that, you file as a single. But what about the family house? If you sell it filing joint, you get $500,000 of capital gains exclusion. If you wait and sell it when filing single, you only get a $250,000 capital gains exclusion. If your home has appreciated significantly, and you don't live in a community property state where the home receives a complete reset in basis, you might be better off either selling it now or, if not, waiting for it to receive the reset in basis in your estate after you join your partner at Forest Lawn.

If you are younger than your departed spouse, your IRA money can be pulled out in smaller increments over your longer remaining projected lifespan. But if you roll your departed spouse's IRA into your IRA, distributions cannot be taken from it without penalty until age 59½. If you are younger and need the income now, leave it as an inherited IRA in your departed spouse's name to keep the RMDs flowing, or calculate what your 72(t) distributions would be to see if those would provide enough income. Follow these rules to the letter to avoid penalties. Alternatively, if the surviving spouse is over 70½, and the deceased spouse is under 70½, the surviving spouse could keep the IRA as an inherited IRA if they did not want to take the RMDs that would click in if they rolled it into their own IRA. This would change to age 72 under the Secure Act.

The issues don't end there. Your income will have fallen with the loss of the smaller Social Security check, and you also say goodbye to half your standard deduction when you file single. The surviving spouse in the cozy cocoon of the 24% bracket under TCJA could suddenly find him or herself in the 35% bracket after the TCJA expires in 2025. Or, transported from 12% bracket to the 25% bracket. All this foretells less income, lower deductions, and higher tax rates. As blogger MD on FIRE puts it, the government has become your new life partner.

These contingencies should be part of your tax and income planning from the beginning of retirement, with an eye toward Roth conversions to shelter income for the surviving spouse. Tax planning should focus on avoiding rising brackets, the Social Security tax torpedo (see below), capital gain bump zones, the 3.8% Obamacare tax, and higher Medicare surtaxes.

* * *

Having reviewed the strategies by life stage, we will now approach the beast according to which tax bracket you inhabit.

The 12% Bracket (or Less)

This honky-tonk is the place to be, tax-wise. You get to use the standard exemptions and deductions and might even be eligible for various tax credits. A single person can be in this bracket with up to $52,525 in income and a married couple with up to $105,050 in 2020. You are in tax Valhalla, and your mission is to stay there.

At the low end, you will want to investigate claiming the Earned Income Tax Credit, the Child and Dependent Care Credit, the Savers Tax Credit, the American Opportunity Tax Credit, and the Lifetime Learning Credit. As economist Frank Knight advised, "Accept all subsidies."

Beyond that, you are unlikely to encounter many tax problems in this zone. Just make sure you are not in a capital gains bump zone and, if retired, are not hit by the Social Security tax torpedo.

The Social Security Tax Torpedo

As identified by William Reichenstein and William Meyer, this refers to a jump in your marginal tax rate that hits where Social

Security income suddenly starts to be taxed and then drops back to normal at a higher income threshold after the upper limit on Social Security taxation is reached. Your marginal tax rate can nearly double. The torpedo starts anywhere between $10,000 and $20,000 of income (excluding Social Security itself) and ends somewhere between $33,000 and $48,000. For marrieds, it starts between $17,000 and $25,000 (excluding Social Security income) and ends somewhere between $47,000 and $67,000.

Are you in this ballpark? You won't know if the tax torpedo strikes you unless you run the numbers. To find out, go to:

https://www.calcxml.com/calculators/how-much-of-my-social-security-benefit-may-be-taxed

After you do the data entry, you will see an orange circle representing the percentage of your Social Security income that is taxed. There are two answers you are looking for: 0% or 85%. Any other number means you are taxed egregiously. Raise or lower your income to one side of the torpedo or the other; don't mess with Mr. In-Between.

Strategy One: If you are under seventy, postpone taking Social Security. In the meantime, draw from your Traditional IRA for living expenses. This will lower your eventual RMD. Your Social Security check, when you finally collect it, will be larger, but only half of it counts towards income. This could lower what Social Security is pleased to call your "preliminary income" to a point where your Social Security check would escape taxation altogether.

Strategy Two: If you have already started the RMDs, then the magic answer is partial Roth conversions. Convert just enough of your Traditional IRA to a Roth IRA to raise your income to the point where 85% of your Social Security income is taxed. That means you have dropped back to the bracket where you belong. Just make sure that you don't cross the $85,000 single/$170,000 married threshold that would raise your Medicare premium along the way.

Strategy Three: The first year you take Social Security, do a big enough Roth conversion to lower your projected RMDs in later years such that you escape the torpedo forever.

Retirement Accounts

To stay in the 12% bracket, maximize contributions to your IRA or 401(k) plan, or, if retired, live off cash savings or pull money from your Roth IRA. Roth income is invisible and can even help you avoid taxes on Social Security income. However, the important thing is to use all of these in a way that minimizes your taxes not only this year but over the long term.

Fund your 401(k) at least to the point where you capture any employer matching contribution. The usual decision tree applies for funding a Roth versus a traditional IRA. If your bracket is higher later, a Roth is better—indeed, this might be your last chance to get into a Roth cheaply if you are climbing the corporate letterhead to the toppermost of the poppermost. Or, convert your traditional IRA to a Roth up to the top of your low bracket.

If you have a high-deductible medical policy, open a Health Savings Account. Pay for current medical outlays out of pocket and let this money compound until late retirement.

The first thing to do is to fill your 0% income tax bracket (which goes up to the amount of your standard deduction, typically) with a partial Roth conversion. Remember that RMDs and Social Security income will also be filling your 0% bracket, along with ordinary income, so that this 0% Roth conversion bracket may get crowded out by your other sources of income and Roth conversions will cost something. However, if you are in the 12% bracket now, you probably will be in the 15% bracket once the TCJA sunsets, so there is little danger in doing Roth conversions now to the top of the 12% bracket.

Taxable Accounts

Apart from nabbing the up-front deduction and a possible employer match, tax-deferred accounts are less valuable to people in the 12% bracket because typically they are not paying a lot of taxes on their investment accounts anyway. Tax management, therefore, involves playing defense against the possibility of higher taxes in the future. Capital gains losses (as they are called) are of only limited use, although the $3,000 of losses that get applied against ordinary income might help, especially on the border of a higher bracket. Otherwise, the correct move is to realize capital gains to keep your cost basis as high as possible. Tell the custodian of your brokerage account to change its accounting method to sell your low-cost shares first, and make sure the realized gains don't push you into a higher bracket. Mutual funds may pile on dividends and capital gains at the end of the year, so leave room for these.

A single person who zeroed out her $12,400 standard deduction with a Roth conversion could additionally realize $40,000 in capital gains and dividends in 2020 if she had no other income and still pay $0 Federal Income Tax. A married couple could double these amounts with no tax owed. That digests a lot of capital gains. Of course, if the securities will never need to be sold for living expenses, there is less point in doing this. It might help in the event the capital gains step-up at death is repealed in the future.

ACA Obamacare Subsidy

If you are relying on the Affordable Care Act exchanges for health insurance and receiving a subsidy, the cutoff is usually at 400% of the Federal Poverty Level. Earn $1 more and the premium subsidy—perhaps $10,000—is gone. The specifics depend on your state of residence and your household size. This cutoff is a number worth keeping in mind. Roth IRA distributions do not count as income when making this calculation.

Because of the inconsistent way the subsidies apply, you should check all the "metal" plans to see which one is the best deal. It may not be the cheapest plan.

The 22% to 24% Tax Brackets

Roth Accounts

Unfortunately, Roth conversions are more expensive at this point. But they can still be advantageous if you avoid higher taxes later. You have a lot of headroom to do Roth conversions within the 24% bracket. You won't know whether these are economically advantageous unless you do the calculations. A backdoor Roth could also work.

Traditional IRAs and 401(k)s et al.

In general, fund these to the top every year because the tax deduction is so valuable. You will likely be in the 25% or the 28% bracket after the TCJA sunsets.

Taxable Accounts

With the ACA Obamacare 3.8% surtax kicking in at $200,000 single/$250,000 married, higher taxes on dividends and capital gains (plus state taxes) all take a toll on your long-term investment performance. Use exchange-traded funds. Rebalance your portfolios in a tax-scrupulous manner. Harvest capital losses whenever they arise to offset gains elsewhere. Tune your brokerage account tax settings to the most tax-sensitive station.

If you are retired and foresee a problem with realized capital gains pushing you from the 15% to the 18.3% capital gains bracket later, capital gain harvesting can forestall this.

The 32%, 35% and 37% Brackets

P.S. these are really the 32.9%, 35.9%, and 37.9% brackets because by now you are paying the Medicare surtax. This is the end of the line. You have reached the shining city on a hill, and now you have to pay for it.

Marriage Penalty

As singles, both of you could earn $1,036,800 before being foist into the 37% bracket. Get married, and your top rate is exacted starting at $622,050. Singles both get to take a $10,000 deduction for state and local taxes, while marrieds have to share it. You can calculate the size of your penalty here:

https://tpc-marriage-calculator.urban.org/

Tax Records

How long should you retain tax records? If you are in a high bracket (i.e., much more likely to be audited), you should keep all records until the time has passed when the IRS might want to examine them. Six years would be good. If you've done anything cute that might capture the attention of a smart government attorney who likes a challenge and has astonishing firepower at his disposal to come after you, keep them forever. At your bracket, you can afford to hire someone to scan all your tax records and supporting documents so you won't have boxes cluttering up your attic.

Roth IRAs

Conversion is expensive but can still pay. The window between now and 2025 may be your last best opportunity. If the Democrats take over both houses of Congress as well as the Presidency 2021, the TCJA may be revoked even sooner.

Otherwise, your best bet is a backdoor Roth for small sums, or fund a post-tax Roth 401(k).

Traditional IRAs and 401(k)s

The deduction today is valuable, but upon the forced withdrawal, your qualified accounts become tax traps spinning the gold of capital gains and dividends into the hay of ordinary income. With no viable relief from Roth conversions, you are stuck.

If you don't need your RMDs for living expenses in retirement, giving up to $100,000 (or $200,000 total for marrieds) as a qualified charitable distribution directly from your IRA custodian might lower your tax bracket, or at least cut your Medicare Part B surcharge.

Whether or not the Secure Act passes, the government has shown its interest in forcing you to empty your retirement accounts as soon as possible so it can tax them. Once your qualified plans exceed a million dollars, consider whether it might be safer to pay the taxes today and park the money in your taxable account instead, where (arguably) it would be harder to confiscate.

Taxable Accounts

You are already paying 23.8% on dividends and capital gains (plus your state taxes on top of this).

This makes intra-account events expensive: interest, dividends, capital gains, turnover within or between funds, and portfolio rebalancing. Tax-loss harvesting is allowed and encouraged, but all other changes should be approached with circumspection.

Once retired, if you need to make withdrawals to cover living expenses, dividends and realized capital gains are fine up to the amount you need—but anything beyond this should be avoided. Harvest all capital losses, realize capital gains only when necessary for consumption, and sell your highest-basis assets first.

One cheap source of income late in life would be to invest in Master Limited Partnerships in your taxable account. Most of the dividends will be a return of principal. If you buy these when you are in your eighties, you probably won't live long enough to see them drawdown to where they have a negative tax basis and the payments are taxed as ordinary income. You can leave them in your estate and let your heirs sell them at the stepped-up basis.

If you are making withdrawals from your taxable account to fund living expenses, consider a portfolio loan instead. The loan itself not taxed, although you do have to pay interest. As long as the loan rate is less than the rate of return on your investments, and provided that you maintain a very, very prudent loan-to-value ratio, this can work better than selling down your account and paying the taxes along the way.

When one spouse dies, the surviving spouse can disclaim the IRA and let it pass directly to the kids as secondary beneficiaries. Suddenly the RMD disappears—it is now the kids' problem (but think twice before disclaiming if the Secure Act has passed and your kids will be looking for financial aid for college within the next decade).

Disclaiming the IRA would make the taxable account more valuable, as now the portfolio can be tapped for living expenses as capital gains rather than at ordinary income tax rates. Unlike the IRA, the taxable account will receive a fair market value reset in cost basis when the surviving spouse departs. A Roth IRA is the bequest asset of choice for high-income kids, but it is hard for high-bracket parents to build up much value in a Roth without paying heavily for the privilege.

The Boneyard

🦴 Riding the brackets means trying to shift income from high-earning years to years when you are in lower brackets, so you spend as little time as possible exposed to the highest rates.

🦴 To avoid the tax bracket creeps, bleed your IRAs early in retirement through a series of partial Roth IRA conversions to keep them from jacking you into higher brackets later.

🦴 When it comes to retirement, you need to solve for everything at once: income, social security, RMDs, expenses, Roth conversions, and taxes. You are going to have to use software to drill down into this and come up with your best plan.

Chapter Six

Zero-Dividend
Investing for Rich Dogs

Here's a nickel history of investing:

- Up through the 1970s, the primary way to invest was through ownership of individual stocks and bonds, hand-selected by your artisanal full-service, high-commission broker.

- In the 1980s, mutual funds flourished. You could pay a single commission and buy an entire portfolio of stocks, run by a rockstar manager who was smarter than your broker.

- By the 1990s, it became clear to intelligent retail investors that passively owning the entire market was usually superior to hiring a rockstar manager. Index mutual funds moved to the head of the class.

- By the 2000s, retail investors realized they could get better performance by capitalizing on predictable market anomalies/inefficiencies. Investment companies like Dimensional Funds offered the small company and value premiums. Other fund companies joined the list, plating up the hot factor du jour: momentum, low volatility, profitability, high quality, and so on.
- Finally, exchange-traded funds (ETFs) mushroomed, bringing obscure and specialized indexes and factor-based strategies to the market.

This mutual fund love fest has an ugly secret locked in the fruit cellar. Morningstar says that typical mutual fund costs middle-bracket taxpayers somewhere between 1% - 1.2% in taxes every year right off the top, but that's not what I'm talking about. Nor am I referring to the embedded capital gains that can get transferred to remaining fund investors from redemptions by those departing. No, I mean there is a kink in the tax code itself.

Mutual funds cannot pass along their internal losses to shareholders. Shareholders get taxed on a fund's gains, but they do not get the full benefit from a fund's losses.

Consider:

- A fund has internal gains that surpass its losses this year. Result: you pay taxes on the gains.
- A fund has internal losses that surpass gains this year. Result: you do not get to deduct the losses from your taxes. You lose it but don't use it.

This is true even if you did not buy or sell a single share of the fund during the year. It is all inside baseball from transactions in the fund itself. Nor does it matter if the fund was a traditional "open-ended" mutual fund, a closed-end fund, a tax-managed fund, or an exchange-traded fund.

In a low-tax world, the problem would not matter very much. But the present tax code imposes high tax rates on high-income investors. It is hard to get ahead when the G-Men and the states take nearly one-third of your profits every year. Meanwhile, the short-term gains or unqualified dividends your fund spits out, are taxed at your marginal rate or even higher.

As I look out from the ramparts, I don't perceive any groundswell to lower taxes on high-income investors. Quite the opposite. The meme is all about soaking the rich to pay for our ever-expanding social programs. Will your alpha manager or your smart beta fund come out ahead after taxes in this sort of world?

High-net-worth families have trouble accumulating much wealth inside tax-advantaged accounts like IRAs. There isn't enough headroom. Their money sloshes over into taxable accounts. From there, it is prey to mismanagement by self-dealing private investment banks and family offices. By the second generation, the family has been scripted for dependency and is relatively clueless about money even if they have learned how to throw some finance lingo around. This makes them doubly ignorant.

It will not shock you to learn that these accounts are run with an eye toward maximum invisible fee extraction and the kickback of favors. The family gets steered into snobby but inscrutable investments like hedge funds and private equity, where their performance proves disappointing while the fees and taxes go through the roof. There are exceptions, but would you expect to be one of them? The ultra-high-net-worth are better advised to skip tax-inefficient asset classes altogether if they cannot be housed in tax-qualified accounts. Yale can invest in these and make money sometimes, but—and I say this with the greatest respect—you ain't Yale.

Here is a typical scenario I came across: an iconic American family figured out they could only sustain their principal by withdrawing 3% from its fund annually: 1% to Wall Street, 1% to the IRS, and 1% to the family. Live it up, kids. This suggests a line of attack: pare back the 1% to Wall Street and the 1% to the IRS.

To move to the next square on the tax game board, reclaim the tax benefits you surrendered to mutual funds. Instead of buying mutual funds, buy individual stocks.

Immediately you regain the ability to use your losses, just like investors did in the 1950s. It's back to the future—but this time with a peppermint twist. You are no longer trying to beat the market. You only are trying to beat Wall Street and the IRS.

How well does this work? Research by John Birge and Song Yang shows that a portfolio containing many assets—even when these assets have a cost basis of zero, so long as they are numerous—can be liquidated to the tune of 3% to 7% annually and still postpone paying any capital gains taxes for ten to fifteen years. When would you prefer to pay your tax bill: now, or ten years from now?

Enter Zero-Dividend Stocks

While a great leap forward, a portfolio of individual stocks takes you only half of the way to capture tax efficiency. Step two is using zero-dividend stocks: not a mutual fund, not an exchange-traded fund, but a diversified portfolio of individual companies that don't pay dividends. This is the portfolio of choice for large taxable accounts of high-income investors.

Why? Because from a tax perspective, receiving a dividend is identical to a forced sale and realization of stock gains with a cost basis of zero—the worst possible case. Dividends make you pay all the taxes this year, also the worst case. With capital appreciation, you pay taxes only when you sell, and even then only on the shares you sell (which could be at a loss or include a substantial untaxed return of principal). If you never sell, the stocks go into your estate and receive the fair market value reset. But dividends receive no step up and so are costly both to you now and to your heirs later (although the cost is invisible to your heirs because they never see the money that was spent needlessly on taxes).

As DiLellio and Ostrov (2019) put it, "Given a choice between two stocks with an expected return of 5%, where one stock returns 4 of that 5% as dividends and the other gives no dividends, the heavy majority of retirees and their advisors will pick the stock that returns dividends for reasons including that dividend paying firms are often considered to be more stable than non-dividend paying firms. From a taxation point of view, however, this is a considerable mistake." How much of a mistake? In their example, for a retiree with a $1 million taxable account, replacing dividend stocks with non-dividend stocks leads to a transfer of an additional $324,889 to the heir.

Buying companies that do not pay dividends effectively converts your taxable account into a de facto IRA:

- Like a Roth IRA, there is no tax deduction going in, but you get permanent tax-free compounding inside the account.

- Like a Roth IRA, there are no mandatory distributions for you (and, unlike with a Roth IRA, there are no mandatory distributions for your heirs).

- Distributions, when you choose to take them, are either untaxed as a straight return of principal or (because held more than one year) they are assessed at more favorable long-term capital gains rates. They are not taxed as ordinary income, as with a traditional IRA.

- Better than a traditional IRA, your heirs get a step-up in cost basis when your canoe shoves off for the Happy Hunting Ground.

- Better than any IRA, you can harvest and use capital gains losses to offset capital gains or even ordinary income to some extent.

- Better than any IRA, you can use these assets as the basis for a portfolio loan. You pay interest on the loan, but not taxes.

- Better than any IRA, there are not a lot of tricky and ever-changing rules to follow that risk severe tax penalties if you make a mistake.
- Better than any IRA, the account passes to beneficiaries through your estate, avoiding the need for a second tier of complicated estate planning.

There are some situations where zero-dividend stocks are already the go-to choice. For example, if your kids are young (and young can mean up to twenty-four years old), any income from their portfolio over $2,200 a year is taxed at trust tax rates. Buying and holding zero-dividend stocks sidesteps this problem.

Another instance: many trusts contain language to the effect that earnings must be distributed to beneficiaries. However, trust earnings often are defined as interest and dividends. You can realize capital gains all day long and not have to take distributions. Or, you can have unrealized capital gains and never pay taxes, which is nice because trust income is taxed at the top marginal rates starting at a super-low $12,950 in 2020. (If the trust does have dividend income, it is most efficient to arbitrage the low ceiling for the trust top tax rates against the higher ceiling for the individual tax rates by distributing trust income to beneficiaries in lower brackets.)

Another: your income subjects you to the 3.8% Obamacare surtax on investment income such as dividends.

And another: you are retired and see that your mandatory IRA distributions are eventually going to create a tax problem. By holding zero-dividend stocks in your taxable accounts, you create more headroom to take larger distributions from other sources without pushing up your bracket.

And still another: you are retired and have a Roth, a Traditional IRA, and a zero-dividend brokerage account. You can use the Roth account to supplement the income from the Traditional IRA, leaving the entire zero-dividend account to receive the step-up in basis in your estate. This transfers more net wealth to your heirs than selling the stocks in the brokerage account for retirement income and paying capital gains taxes along the way. With dividend stocks, you are always paying taxes along the way.

Zero-dividend stocks are the preferred investment choice for the taxable portfolios of high-earning, very-high-net-worth investors.

I got this idea from my guru, Warren Buffett. While Warren occasionally speaks about the benefits of the rich paying more taxes, and always talks up how much tax Berkshire Hathaway pays, he is a walking encyclopedia of the tax code and plays it like a fiddle.

How good is Buffett? In 2010, Buffett had a net worth of $71 billion, taxable income of $39.8 million, and paid $6.9 million in taxes. As *Barron*'s noted, "Proportionately, that's like someone with an ever-expanding net worth, currently $10 million, reporting taxable income of only $5,000 and paying a federal tax bill of only $900."

Buffett's 2012 *Letter to Shareholders* discusses the problem of dividends and presents the following example:

Imagine you own a company worth $1,000,000. This business earns 12% annually on its net value, and its shares trade at 1.25× this value in the stock market.

You decide you would like the company to pay a 4% dividend every year. Because it earns 12% on net value, that leaves 8% inside the company to compound. Let us follow this happy scenario to its conclusion over a decade (Table 6.1).

	Business net value	Business market value	You own	Your shares	Annual dividends
TABLE 6.1 Take the dividend					
Start	$1,000,000	$1,250,000	100%	$1,250,000	–
Year 1	$1,080,000	$1,350,000	100%	$1,350,000	$40,000
Years 2-9	. . .	. . .	. . .	. . .	. . .
Year 10	$2,158,925	$2,698,656	100%	$2,698,656	$79,960
Finish	$2,158,925	$2,698,656	100%	**$2,698,656**	**$579,462**

Over the decade, you pulled out $579,462 in dividends. You haven't sold a single share. If you sold the business today, you would pocket $2,698,656.

As felicitous as that sounds, Buffett claims you could have done better. How? Instead of taking the dividend, you could have raised the same amount of cash by breaking off and selling a little piece of your stock holding every year along the way. Watch what happens then (Table 6.2):

TABLE 6.2 Sell the stock					
	Business net value	Business market value	You own	Your shares	Annual sell-off
Start	$1,000,000	$1,250,000	100%	$1,250,000	–
Year 1	$1,120,000	$1,400,000	96.8%	$1,355,200	$40,000
Years 2-9	. . .	. . .	. . .	. . .	. . .
Year 10	$3,105,848	$3,882,310	72.2%	$2,804,425	$110,923
Total	$3,105,848	$3,882,310	72.2%	**$2,803,028**	**$701,949**

Notice how your situation has improved. You pulled out 21% more cash ($701,949 vs. $579,462) by creating your own 4% "synthetic dividend" via stock sales over the decade. As a result, you now own fewer shares of the company (72.2% vs. 100% in the first example); however, the business has become more valuable as a result of your having left more money inside it to compound. If you sold it today, you would net $2,803,028 vs. $2,698,656 in the first example (3.9% more). You had your cake and ate it, too: more cash along the way and a more valuable stock holding in the end. This explains why Berkshire Hathaway doesn't pay a dividend.

Buffett adds that dividends equal forced taxation since you pay the tax whether you need the dividend or not. The more parsimonious approach is for shareholders to sell just enough stock to raise any cash they need. That way, there are no taxes beyond those absolutely necessary. Depending on which shares the investor chooses to sell, the proceeds could represent a return of principal at no tax, capital gains at capital gains tax rates, or some blend of the two.

Tax-wise, zero-dividend stocks are a no-brainer. But do they make sense as an investment?

How Do Zero-Dividend Stocks Perform?

Ronen Israel and Toby Moskowitz of AQR Capital examined the stock market from July 1974 through June 2010. They compared the returns of the zero-dividend stocks in the index to the returns of the S&P 500 and Russell 1000 indexes as a whole, after taxing both portfolios at 2011 rates (35% on short-term gains, 15% on long-term gains and dividends) each year over thirty-six years (Table 6.3).

TABLE 6.3 Index versus zero-dividend stocks after-tax returns			
	After-tax index return	"Zero-dividend" return	Difference
S&P 500	9.73%	10.19%	0.47%
Russell 1000	9.84%	10.08%	0.24%

What did they discover? *The after-tax returns of the zero-dividend S&P 500 and Russell 1000 over this thirty-six-year period were higher than the after-tax returns of the original indexes.* If you paid more than a 15% tax on dividends, your relative returns would have been even higher.

Another finding was that excluding dividend stocks meant the remaining portfolio did not track the index very closely. This is hardly surprising because most stocks do pay a dividend, such that a no-dividend mandate can eliminate 60% to 80% of the stocks in the index. Tracking error to the benchmark makes some investors uneasy. There is comfort in knowing you are in the same boat with everyone else.

Columbia professor Andrew Ang's investment textbook presents a straightforward example, starring a hypothetical stock mutual fund earning 12% every year versus a zero-dividend stock earning the same. Both are held in taxable accounts with the earnings taxed at 15% (Table 6.4).

		TABLE 6.4 After-tax portfolio growth		
Year	Mutual fund	Zero-dividend stock	Outperformance
0	$1,000	$1,000	0%
10	$2,641	$2,790	6%
20	$6,976	$8,349	20%
30	$19,824	$25,616	29%

Ang's conclusion: "The most important lesson is to save in a way that is sheltered from taxes. Everything else is secondary." He adds, "Warren Buffett is right not to pay dividends."

Which Zero-Dividend Stocks?

As Chairman Buffett noted in his 1993 letter, "tax-paying investors will realize a far, far greater sum from a single investment that compounds internally than from a succession of investments compounding at the same rate."

We need to buy companies with staying power. When Ben Stein and I were in Warren's office, he put it like this: imagine you were leaving town for ten years to sail around the world. What would you buy if you knew you couldn't check on your holdings?

That is the perspective here. We are looking for large, stable, high-quality businesses to buy and hold forever. Ideally, businesses that have long runways for expansion and opportunities to deploy new capital.

The Zero-Dividend Portfolio

Some people have made Berkshire Hathaway their entire investment portfolio. They didn't intend to, but early investors found that it kept growing and growing until it crowded out everything else. I met a Buffett family babysitter from the 1960s who put all her money with Warren, and she is now an extremely wealthy women.

While Berkshire, a holding company, is a zero-dividend stock, some of the companies it owns pay dividends to it. These are taxed internally at 11%–13%, which is less than you would pay if they were passed through.

Berkshire has gone down in price by half on three occasions over its history. More diversification is in order. A selection of quality businesses from a variety of industries, bought at reasonable prices, should allow investors to participate in the growth of the global economy over the coming decades. Twenty (or more) companies that are equally weighted give diversification a chance to work and harvesting losses along the way to offset the gains. Researchers estimate that this opportunity is worth about 5% to 6% per decade compared to holding a single index fund. This is like getting a free extra year of retirement income for every decade you invest.

Most investors will not build their entire portfolios out of zero-dividend stocks, even after reading this book. They have retirement accounts where these rules don't apply, and they have preexisting holdings in their taxable accounts that pay dividends but have become too expensive to sell. Or, they don't want to make an all-in bet on any one strategy. Even so, a "completion" portfolio of zero-dividend stocks makes sense. The idea would be to pick zero-dividend stocks going forward to round out their portfolios while doing no further harm to their tax status.

The tax alpha dog aims for a zero-turnover portfolio. He buys and holds forever. Unless he needs liquidity, he only sells to recognize tax losses. These he chases down like rabbits.

Taxes levied on portfolio turnover are the great self-inflicted gunshot wound of portfolio returns. Using data lifted from Michael Kitces, Figure 6.1 shows the impact of dividends and turnover on a $100,000 portfolio over thirty years under a regime of 7.5% returns and a 15% dividend and capital gains tax (remember your taxes could be twice that high).

FIGURE 6.1.
Impact of dividends and portfolio turnover

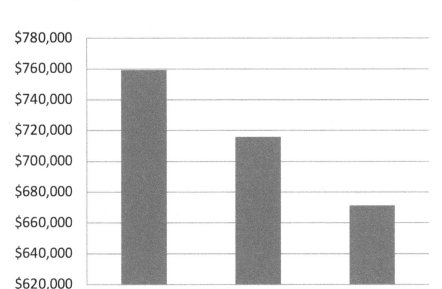

The tall column shows how much your money grows after all taxes with no dividends or portfolio turnover—the tax alpha way. The middle column shows how much that amount shrinks if the portfolio pays a 2.5% dividend annually. Finally, the short column includes both dividends and a 10% realization of capital gains every year. The typical mutual fund has an annual turnover of 85%. It would fall off the page.

No wonder the Voya Corporate Leaders Trust Fund has out-performed 98% of its peers. It bought thirty stocks in 1935 and hasn't picked a new one since. Similarly, Fidelity Investments found that its best-performing portfolios belonged to clients who were dead—the ultimate passive investors.

Objections

You fool! You give up the diversification of owning the entire market.

You should either own a large number of zero-dividend stocks or choose carefully among them to maximize your internal portfolio diversification. Statistically, once you get past owning twenty stocks, the diversification benefits of adding each additional stock thin out (although the opportunities for tax-loss harvesting increase).

A more trenchant criticism would be this: your zero-dividend stock portfolio will not reflect the underlying structure of the global economy. Some industries (technology) will be overrepresented, while others (utilities) will be underrepresented. It will underweight foreign stocks, almost all of which pay dividends. You could make up the difference in your other holdings (say, inside your IRA) or live with the difference as the price you pay for escaping taxation.

Over the long run, we expect to reap the returns of equity investing, but with no expectation of matching the indexes year to year. We are trading benchmark tracking uncertainty for low tax certainty. The right attitude is to play golf and check your portfolio as seldom as possible, knowing that we are doing the best we can for our families over the long run by not paying the government today. There will always be different approaches that perform better, identified after the fact, but we have no way of knowing which Bingo numbers will win next year.

What if a no-dividend company starts issuing dividends?

At that point, we would have to weigh the tax consequences of remaining invested and keeping the dividend versus the tax costs of selling and moving on to another non-dividend payer. For long-term holdings, most of the time it probably will be cheaper to live with the stock, dividends and all. We will have received the benefit of however many years of tax-free compounding. It is not about arriving at some permanent plateau of perfection; it's about deferring taxes as best we can.

What if Congress decides to tax unrealized capital gains?

Then it's game over—or, maybe not. It could change back at the next election. Tax policy experts think taxing unrealized gains is a dumb idea. The current policy of not taxing unrealized gains dates back to 1921, and there are excellent reasons for not changing it, but anything is possible. It is best not to make a 100% bet on any one strategy.

A more likely prospect would be for Congress to eliminate the fair market value reset at death, and so require heirs to carry forward the cost basis of inherited securities. Per usual, this would raise less revenue than anticipated, as the heirs would adapt by borrowing against rather than selling assets to meet spending requirements. It would, however, have the stultifying effect of freezing capital deployment in less productive assets, with negative implications for the rest of the economy.

Won't I get better results from "factor" investing: value, momentum, etc.?

Possibly.

For people in high brackets, zero-dividend investing is the new factor. Traditional factor investing leads to higher portfolio turnover than we want, which ideally is none (apart from tax-loss harvesting).

There is also no reason why an investor can't do both. For example, use a factor approach for one part of her portfolio (in tax-deferred or tax-exempt accounts) and a tax alpha approach in her taxable account. Adding judiciously selected zero-dividend stocks to an existing portfolio almost invariably will increase diversification, lowering the overall risk profile to some degree.

Or try this: Meb Faber (along with Wes Gray and Jack Vogel) found that simply eliminating the top 25% of dividend payers significantly increased the returns of a value-tilted portfolio, 1974–2015, even pre-tax.

For people paying 0% on their capital gains and dividends, this strategy offers no advantages. But for people in high brackets, an allocation to zero-dividend stocks would be a smart factor to follow in its own right.

Haven't you written lovingly about the wisdom of dividend stocks in the past (you hypocrite)?

Yes, especially in *The Affluent Investor*. A retiree who selects low-volatility/high-quality/high-dividend stocks will experience more stable cash flows than one who relies exclusively on capital gains. These dividend stocks generally should be held inside an IRA.

Won't the portfolio be boxed in with huge capital gains over time? Aren't you just setting us up for a taxpocoplyse later?

Yes, that is exactly the plan. Over decades, the weaklings will be culled from the herd for their tax losses and your unrealized capital gains will grow. When sales are made, the highest-basis shares will be selected, banishing the unrealized gains to the distant future. Why? Because the longer capital gains are postponed, the greater the value you derive from deferring them. The more we defer, the longer we wait, and the higher the taxes we pay, the more valuable this method becomes.

If all goes well, eventually our portfolio will grow into a Scrooge McDuck money bin of capital gains. We will burn through all our capital losses, plus have the original cost basis from our stocks returned to us at no tax, leaving nothing but unrealized capital appreciation that will turn into gold when our heirs collect the giant step-up in cost basis. That means we have completely optimized the tax utility of our taxable portfolio.

As the tax alpha dog looks over his statements for the last time, he will say with satisfaction, "Tis a far, far better Form 1099-DIV than I have ever filed; 'tis a far, far better rest that I go to than I have ever known."

The Boneyard

⬿ Mutual funds do not let investors fully capitalize on losses that occur within the funds. You regain this ability when you use individual stocks.

- High tax rates make dividend stocks expensive for high-earning investors, both now and in retirement.
- A diversified portfolio of buy-and-hold, zero-dividend stocks offers excellent after-tax prospects for high-income dogs seeking to build generational family wealth.

Chapter Seven

Putting the Leash
on Estate Taxes

Prudence dictates that we give some thought to the possibility—however remote—that we might one day depart this dim, vast vale of tears on that last night train to Elvisville.

Here is the estate tax in three bullets:

- You get an $11.58 million estate tax exemption, indexed for inflation. If you prefer, you can use this same amount during life for a gift
- Your spouse can use your unused portion (aka "portability")
- The estate (or gift) tax rate beyond this exemption: 40%

Now only the very high-net-worth will pay the estate tax—possibly less than 0.1% of Americans.

Before 2012, with a small exemption and high estate tax rates (55%), the whole idea was to get assets out of your estate so they wouldn't be taxed. Today, with a big exemption and lower estate tax rates (40%), the best plan for most people is to keep their assets inside their estates.

This means estate planning now harmonizes with retirement planning. Under the new tax regime, job one is maximizing your step-up in cost basis at kick-off time. Apart from a concentrated low-cost-basis holding such as a family business, the best way for most people to extract the maximum juice from the new law is by holding a long-term portfolio of zero-dividend stocks. By borrowing against or selling your highest basis assets for living expenses during retirement, minimizing your taxes then, you effectively tee up your lowest-cost-basis assets for step-up after your departure, minimizing taxes later.

For the 99.9%

It used to be that everybody had the same will—the one with the bypass trust going to the surviving spouse funded with an amount equal to the applicable federal exclusion. That's out. You don't want that anymore. Forget about avoiding federal estate taxes and just set up your estate so that the assets go where you want them to go. This is a considerable improvement.

The next step is to check all your beneficiary forms. Most people's inheritance does not pass through their will or estate plan at all—it passes through the beneficiary forms from their retirement accounts, life insurance policies, annuities, employee benefit plans and stock options. Are you morally certain that yours have been filed correctly and reflect your current intentions?

It's all about the basis

We want everything included in the estate to get the step-up in cost basis (where the cost basis of your assets gets reset to the fair market value when you die, eliminating their embedded capital gains liability).

Not all assets benefit equally. To the extent that you want to spend some now and save others for your estate, Table 7.1 gives the rundown.

Intellectual property includes patents, copyrights, trademarks, or works of art that you have created. These typically have a cost basis close to zero. If you sell them, you realize enormous capital gains. If you license them, you are handed back ordinary income taxed at your marginal rate. If you try to give them away, your zero-cost basis sticks to them like a stamp to a letter. But your heirs will receive them with a step-up in basis.

TABLE 7.1 Freebasing
Very valuable
Intellectual property
Negative-basis assets
Oil & Gas Investments
Collectibles
Low-basis assets
Ho-hum
High basis stock & bonds
Roth IRA
Cash
Less than zero
Capital gains losses
Annuities
Traditional IRAs & 401(k)s
Health Savings Accounts

Commercial real estate is normally taxed at a 25% capital gains rate. That apartment complex you own that's worth $500,000 but if you sold you would have to recognize $700,000 in capital gains due to the depreciation recapture? Your heirs can now sell it and keep the money. MLPs and negative-basis hedge funds also benefit from the step-up.

Collectibles include art, wine, Barbie dolls, coins, and even precious metal bullion. These are taxed ordinarily at their own special 28% capital gains rate. Now they can be sold for 0% capital gains.

All our low-basis stock gets an instant step-up, vaporizing whatever our capital gains tax rate would have been (23.8% Federal plus state taxes for high earners).

Cash always has a cost basis equal to its face value, and Roth IRAs receive no step-up.

Qualified retirement plans and annuities receive no step-up in basis and continue to have a future tax liability embedded in their bowels. Spend them now if your tax rate is lower than your heirs'. As Jonathon Clements points out, the real death tax facing most Americans is money sitting in their IRAs, which will be taxed as ordinary income to their kids. The best practice is for the IRA taxes to be paid by whoever has the lower overall tax burden—either you or your heirs.

Other Ideas

- Your family limited partnership or limited liability company—the one you set up to get a discount on your estate taxes due to illiquidity and a lack of control? Undo this and put all those assets, naked, back into your estate up to the amount of the exemption. Otherwise, the Feds will turn the gun around and hold the discount against you, giving you only a discounted step-up, not the full amount.

- The same applies to your bypass trust. Unless this was needed for some legitimate nontax reason (fear of spousal remarriage to a tennis instructor or cocktail waitress, a blended family, undue influence, incompetence, asset protection, rapidly appreciating assets, etc.), you want these assets back inside your estate to join the cost basis step-up party.

- If you set up a qualified personal residence trust (QPRT) to get your house to your kids cheaply, this turns out to be another bad idea, because your kids will not get the step-up in basis on the house, which is now the better deal. Figure out if there is some way you can void it, possibly by breaking the terms of the trust.

- Those annual gifts of shares of the family business to the kids, to get the appreciating assets out of your estate? Don't bother. They will do better to inherit them with a full step-up later.

- You don't need that life insurance policy you bought to pay estate taxes. There aren't going to be any estate taxes. You can let it lapse, or if it is a whole life policy, sell it in the aftermarket.

- Whatever you have going on, make sure to consult with your attorney when it comes to undoing the previous plan. This is like defusing a Claymore mine—it needs to be done carefully.

However, just when you can hit the snooze button with the new federal estate tax, here is the rug-pull.

States Are All Over the Map

Where do you plan to die? Even if you escape from Les Federales, some states have estate or inheritance taxes (or both) that are "decoupled" from the federal rates. If you live in one of these, your planning shifts from the Federal to the state level.

Table 7.2 shows the possible estate taxes you might face.

Next question: where do your heirs live? Even if you pay no state taxes on the bequests, they may have to pay taxes when they receive them, as shown in Table 7.3.

Your clever estate planning for Florida will be thrown into a cocked hat if you decide to move to be near the kids in Maryland. Don't buy real estate in one of these states, even if your primary residence is in a no-tax state. Some of these will take the total value of your estate into consideration when taxing you on the real estate you own inside their borders, just to push its value over their exemption limits.

TABLE 7.2 Estate taxes by state		
State	Exemption	Top Rate
Connecticut	$3,600,000	12%
Hawaii	$5.490,000	16%
Illinois	$4,000,000	16%
Maine	$5,600,000	16%
Maryland	$5,000,000	16%
Massachusetts	$1,000,000	16%
Minnesota	$2,700,000	16%
New York	$5,749,000	16%
Oregon	$1,000,000	16%
Rhode Island	$1,561,719	16%
Vermont	$2,750,000	16%
Washington	$2,193,000	20%
D.C.	$5,600,000	12%

TABLE 7.3 Inheritance taxes by state	
State	Range
Iowa	15%
Kentucky	16%
Maryland	16%
Nebraska	18%
New Jersey	16%
Pennsylvania	15%

A better place to retire would be a community property state where joint assets of both parties get stepped up at the death of both spouses. The ones with no state income tax are Texas, Nevada, and Alaska (by correct titling of the assets).

The bad news is that an abyss has opened between the best planning for the Feds versus the states where this decoupling has occurred. There is no general solution. You and your estate attorney will have to hammer out the best strategy.

Timing is important because some states have a "gift-in-contemplation-of-death" rule that can void the gift and make it taxable anyway (Indiana, Iowa, Kentucky, Maryland, Nebraska, Pennsylvania). If you live in one of these, find out what your state's specific practice is. The general advice is to live three more years after you make this kind of arrangement. Set these up well before you head for the departure gate.

Are You Borderline?

If the size of your estate would make it borderline-taxable today, consider that your investments may not grow faster than inflation once you take your future withdrawals into account.

Still, if you are worried that you might reach this point, then you use the standard bag of tricks to get rid of your money:

- Convert your IRA to a Roth if your tax bracket is the same or lower than your kids'. The taxes you pay are out of your estate. There is no "in contemplation of death" clawback rule—the government is always happy to take your tax money today.

- Set up an irrevocable life insurance trust (ILIT) and use your $15,000 annual gifts to buy a (second-to-die) guaranteed no-lapse universal life insurance policy for the trust beneficiaries.

- Fund 529 plans. You and your spouse can use the five-year initial funding to drop $150,000 into each of your kids' or grandkids' accounts. Outlive the five years, or else the remaining money gets clawed back into your estate.

- Give $15,000 annual gifts to everyone else. Appreciated and appreciating securities are great gifts to those in lower tax brackets.

- Pay college tuition directly to the school, even if you have already funded a 529 plan. Tuition dollars are not included in your $15,000 annual exclusion.

- Pay medical expenses for anyone you want by writing checks directly to the medical providers. You can pay for their health insurance this way as well.

You'll be amazed how fast the money spends once you put your back into it.

What to Do with Your IRA if the Secure Act has Passed

If your IRA is $500,000 or less, it will probably be consumed during your lifetime and any residual amount inherited is unlikely to present a tax burden for your heirs.

If you have a larger IRA that will be inherited by someone, your estate tax-planning goal is to shrink the mandatory distributions by (a) stretching the distributions over as long a period as possible, and/or (b) breaking the IRA into smaller pieces so that the resulting distributions are less likely to cause tax bracket creep. This is not easy to do, because most of us will die when we are old, our spouses are old, and our children are grown.

The most likely person to stretch your IRA distributions could be your surviving spouse, depending on your respective ages, assuming you both die on schedule. The downside is that your spouse would be filing as a single taxpayer, so the IRA distributions could be taxed in higher brackets during this period. Listing the children as secondary beneficiaries gives your spouse the option of disclaiming some or all of the IRA if the kids are in lower brackets.

One way in to break up the Traditional IRA into bite-size pieces is to leave $19,000 worth of IRA assets to each of your young grandchildren or great-grandchildren. Note that if a child's income is $2,200 or less in 2020, that child can file his own tax return and pay taxes (if any) at his or her own rates, escaping the kiddie tax. If $19,000 of an Inherited IRA were to go to a grandchild at age 14, and the proceeds appreciated 5% per year with a modest 2% annual inflation, the child would still be able to file his own tax return by age 24 while pulling out the maximum dollar amount allowed under the kiddie tax exclusion. The custodian/parent might be able to fine-tune the distribution by controlling the stock/bond/cash ratio inside the IRA. This is a nuisance, but such is the price of tax minimization. The parents could direct the distribution to a UTMA/UGMA where the money is spent for the child's welfare or directed to a 529 Plan for college expenses.

Stretching under the Secure Act

The Secure Act kills the beloved stretch IRA, which allowed us to leave IRAs (both Roth and Traditional, as well as other qualified plans like 401(k)s and 403(b)s) to our heirs and let them pull out the proceeds over their actuarial lifetimes. Now, our beneficiaries (other than a spouse, a minor child, someone disabled or chronically ill, or someone fewer than ten years younger than we are) are required to pull the money out over ten years. This includes grandchildren.

The net effect is to make more of your IRA subject to higher taxes sooner, as the money is forced out in bigger chunks subject to higher tax rates under our progressive tax system.

Conduit Trusts and Discretionary Trusts

Under the old regime, many taxpayers wanted to leave their IRAs to their young children or grandchildren to take advantage of the long-term tax-free compounding. For obvious reasons, they did not want to give teenagers access to large sums of money, so their attorneys arranged for the RMDs to go into a conduit (or "see-through") trust where they would be available but cashing out the IRA motherload was not an option.

But under the Secure Act there are no more required minimum distributions. The trust would receive nothing until year ten, at which point the entire IRA would be distributed and all the money paid to the kids while being taxed at the highest possible rates—*precisely the opposite of what the parents intended.*

If your qualified plans list a trust as a beneficiary, this requires your immediate attention if the Secure Act has passed.

You could change the trust from a "see-through" trust (where the income is distributed every year) to a discretionary or accumulation trust where a wise trustee can parcel out the money as she sees fit. The problem is that money would be taxed at the stratospheric trust tax rates, where the 37% bracket starts at only $12,950 of income. This could only work for a Roth IRA (although the earnings inside the trust would be still be taxed. Personally, I would not care to be the trustee of a discretionary trust, since keeping the beneficiaries happy would be a minefield. These trusts are also great candidates for abuse since the trustee can elect to keep the money inside the trust and milk it indefinitely for fees and favor kickbacks from his pals, the trust attorney, accountant, and banker/investment advisor. At a minimum, discretionary trusts require trust protector provisions.

In some cases, it is possible to set up a trust out-of-state to receive the IRA distributions and avoid paying taxes on them in your home state. This might work currently if you live in Colorado, Indiana, Kansas, Kentucky, Mississippi, or South Carolina.

Roth vs. Insurance

While Roth IRAs make wonderful bequests for high-income children, the question arises whether you would be better off using the money spent paying taxes on a Roth conversion to liquidate the Traditional IRA and use the proceeds to buy a universal life insurance policy inside an Irrevocable Life Insurance Trust for your beneficiaries. That money is out of your estate and the proceeds from this ILIT would be tax-free to your heirs. While I have seen this idea touted by the insurance industry, I have yet to see a real-world example where this is economically advantageous. Pay for an impartial analysis from someone who is not trying to sell you an insurance policy before signing on for this one.

Using a CRUT

Rich families with large IRAs and some measure of charitable intent might consider making a Charitable Remainder Unit Trust (CRUT) the beneficiary of their traditional IRA. This maneuver can reconstruct the stretch provisions of the inherited IRA that the Secure Act destroyed. The CRUT needs to file a tax return every year but offers you the flexibility to set it up and invest it yourself. The final charity could be your family donor-advised fund (although not your private family foundation). There are plenty of ways to screw this up so you would want to talk it through in advance with your custodian to make sure everything was in good order—especially the beneficiary forms. Major charities are happy to let you invest in CRUTs they manage if you are willing to leave the money to them.

The CRUT swallows all the IRA assets in one gulp but does not pay taxes because it is, after all, a charity. The CRUT looks up the amount of the total gift that goes to charity in a table and the estate gets to use that amount as a tax deduction—10% at a minimum. Meanwhile, the beneficiaries take out, say, 5% per year and pay taxes on that as ordinary income for twenty years. If the CRUT is invested successfully, beneficiaries could even burn through the basis and end up receiving distributions as capital gains at lower tax rates.

For the 0.1%

Death is not the end. There remains the litigation over your estate.

For the ultra-high-net-worth, the goal is the same as it ever was: get assets out of the estate. Estate plan the Sam Walton way, by giving it away before it's worth a lot. The circumstances with families like yours are specific and require customization.

If you use the $11.58 million gift exemption now, the IRS says they will not come after it if the law changes to a less generous exemption in the future. They are handing you a golden opportunity on a silver platter. For example, you could set up a dynasty trust to shift the growth downstream. I would have my estate attorney on speed dial in case the Democrats win the Presidency and Congress in 2020 since you will have about six weeks until the end of 2020 to use what will probably be the best gift opportunity that you will see in your lifetime.

The Boneyard

- Postpone marriage until shortly before death.
- Your million-dollar IRA may have become a highly problematic asset to leave to beneficiaries if the Secure Act has passed.
- In nearly all cases, the portable $11.58 million exemption will take care of your estate tax.
- Your home state may not be bought off so easily, though.
- Get thee to a probate attorney, if for no other reason than to undo the old will you drafted during the Coolidge administration.
- But be prepared to act fast if the Democrats take over the government in 2020.

Afterword

Thank you for reading this book. I hope you have learned some things that will save you a few pennies on your investment taxes.

Most Americans:

- worry about things that they cannot control, like investment returns, instead of things that they can control, like the taxes they will pay on their investments
- do not set up their investment accounts correctly
- do not maximize their retirement account contributions
- do not manage all their accounts on a household basis
- do not hold the right assets in the right accounts
- sell their winners and hang on to their losers
- actively trade their taxable accounts, chasing performance that has left the station
- bet on managers instead of using passive market index funds
- draw down their retirement accounts in the wrong order
- fail to exploit the statutory tax shelters open to them
- do not make long-term tax projections
- have an out-of-date estate plan (if they have one at all)

Getting these fundamentals right can add years of risk-free income to your retirement and leave more money for your kids to inherit. You may not be Lassie or Rin Tin Tin, but truly you will have become a Tax Alpha Dog.

Does it really save you money? The white papers I read on the supposed tax savings invariably strike me as being too optimistic. Below is my guesstimate, based on eyeballing the research and jiggling the dials to bring the numbers down to earth. They are more conservative than estimates you will find touted by the financial services industry.

We'll consider three scenarios: a low-bracket investor with most of his money invested in retirement accounts, a middle-bracket investor with his money evenly split between retirement accounts and taxable accounts, and a high-bracket investor with most of his money in taxable accounts. The strategies don't cover all the tax-saving ideas, but they include some of the important ones that are commonly available. Table A.1 estimates how much money this might save each investor on $100,000 over ten years in. High-bracket investors have the most to gain from careful tax management because they are the ones who pay most of the taxes in the first place. On the other hand, the money saved by low-bracket investors might be more meaningful relative to their income. Whatever your bracket, this is free walking-around money you collect for being smart about your taxes.

TABLE A.1 Projected Tax Savings	
Strategy	**Tax Alpha**
Low-bracket investor	
Index Fund versus active management	0.00%
Optimized asset location	0.00%
Maximize retirement contributions	0.11%
Optimize withdrawal strategy	0.27%
Annual Tax Alpha	0.37%
Free Money on $100,000 in 10 Years	$3,811
Middle-bracket investor	
Index Fund versus active management	0.35%
Optimized asset location	0.23%
Maximize retirement contributions	0.12%
Optimize withdrawal strategy	0.27%
Annual Tax Alpha	0.97%
Free Money on $100,000 in 10 Years	$10,173
High-bracket investor	
Aggressive tax-loss harvesting	0.21%
Zero turnover versus index fund	0.51%
Zero dividend versus index fund	0.68%
Optimized asset location	0.23%
Maximize retirement contributions	0.18%
Optimize withdrawal strategy	0.27%
Annual Tax Alpha	2.08%
Free Money on $100,000 in 10 Years	$22,863

About the Author

Phil DeMuth was the valedictorian of his class at the University of California at Santa Barbara in 1972, and then went on for his master's in communication and Ph.D. in clinical psychology before anyone could stop him. A psychologist and investment advisor, Phil has written for the *Wall Street Journal, Barron's, Forbes,* the *Journal of Financial Planning,*

Photo: Michael Berger

Human Behavior and *Psychology Today* (and anyone else who will dare to publish him), and is the author of nine books on investing, most co-authored with his pal, economist Ben Stein. His opinions have been quoted in the *New York Times,* the *Financial Times, Yahoo! Finance, On Wall Street, Fortune, Research Magazine, Investor's Business Daily, Motley Fool, theStreet.com* and he has been seen on various TV shows, including CNBC's *Worldwide Exchange,*

On the Money, *Squawk Box* and *Closing Bell*, as well as *Fox & Friends*, *Wall Street Week*, and *Consuelo Mack WealthTrack*.

Phil runs Conservative Wealth Management LLC, an investment advisor to high-net-worth families across the country.

Website: www.phildemuth.com

CPSIA information can be obtained
at www.ICGtesting.com
Printed in the USA
LVHW110832161220
672724LV00034B/98/J